NOTES

including
- *Life of the Author*
- *List of Characters*
- *Brief Plot Synopsis*
- *Summaries and Commentaries*
- *Questions for Review*
- *Selected Bibliography*

by
James L. Roberts, Ph.D.
Department of English
University of Nebraska

INCORPORATED

LINCOLN, NEBRASKA   68501

Editor	Consulting Editor
Gary Carey, M.A.	*James L. Roberts, Ph.D.*
University of Colorado	*Department of English*
	University of Nebraska

ISBN 0-8220-0762-2
© Copyright 1986
by
Cliffs Notes, Inc.
All Rights Reserved
Printed in U.S.A.

1994 Printing

Cliffs Notes, Inc.   Lincoln, Nebraska

CONTENTS

LORD JIM
Notes

LIFE OF THE AUTHOR

Joseph Conrad was born Teodor Jozef Konrad Korzeniowski on December 3, 1857, the only child of a patriotic Polish couple living in the southern Polish Ukraine. Conrad's father was esteemed as a translator of Shakespeare, as well as a poet and a man of letters in Poland, and Conrad's mother was a gentle, well-born lady with a keen mind but frail health.

When Conrad was five, his father was arrested for allegedly taking part in revolutionary plots against the Russians and was exiled to northern Russia; Conrad and his mother went with him. His mother died from the hardships of prison life three years later; she was only thirty-four.

Conrad's father sent him back to his mother's brother for his education, and Conrad was never to see him again. The poet-patriot lived only four more years. Conrad was eleven years old, but the emotional bond between him and his father was so strong that a deep melancholy settled within the young boy; much of his writing as an adult is marked by a melancholy undercurrent.

Conrad received a good education in Cracow, Poland, and after a trip through Italy and Switzerland, he decided not to return to his father's homeland. Poland held no promise; already Conrad had suffered too much from the country's Russian landlords. Instead, the young lad decided on a career very different from what one might expect of a boy brought up in Poland; he chose the sea as his vocation.

Conrad reached Marseilles in October of 1874, when he was seventeen, and for the next twenty years, he sailed almost continually. Not surprisingly, most of his novels and short stories have the sea as a background for the action and as a symbolic parallel for their heroes' inner turbulence. In fact, most of Conrad's work concerns the sea. There is very little old-fashioned "romance" in his novels.

Part of this romantic void may be due to the fact that while Conrad was in Marseilles and only seventeen, he had his first love affair. It ended in disaster. For some time, Conrad told people that he had been wounded in a duel, but now it seems clear that he tried to commit suicide.

Conrad left Marseilles in April of 1878, when he was twenty-one, and it was then that he first saw England. He knew no English, but he signed on an English ship making voyages between Lowestoft and Newcastle. It was on that ship that he began to learn English.

At twenty-four, Conrad was made first mate of a ship that touched down in Singapore, and it was here that he learned about an incident that would later become the kernel of the plot for *Lord Jim*. Then, four years later, while Conrad was aboard the *Vidar*, he met Jim Lingard, the sailor who would become the physical model for Lord Jim; in fact, all the men aboard the *Vidar* called Jim "Lord Jim."

In 1886, when Conrad was twenty-nine, he became a British subject, and the same year, he wrote his first short story, "The Black Mate." He submitted it to a literary competition, but it was unsuccessful. This failure, however, did not stop him from continuing to write. During the next three years, in order to fill empty, boring hours while he was at sea, Conrad began his first novel, *Almayer's Folly*. In addition, he continued writing diaries and journals when he transferred onto a Congo River steamer the following year, making notes that would eventually become the basis for one of his masterpieces, *Heart of Darkness*.

Conrad's health was weakened in Africa, and so he returned to England to recover his strength. Then, in 1894, when Conrad was thirty-seven, he returned to sea; he also completed *Almayer's Folly*. The novel appeared the following year, and Conrad married Jessie George, a woman seventeen years his junior. She was a woman with no literary or intellectual interests, but Conrad continued to write with intense, careful seriousness. *Heart of Darkness* was serialized in *Blackwood's Magazine,* and soon after it appeared as a single volume, Conrad turned his time to *Lord Jim*; it would be his twelfth work of fiction.

After only a cursory reading of *Lord Jim*, it is almost impossible to believe that its author did not learn English until he was twenty-one. The novel has a philosophical depth that is profound and a vocabulary that is rich and exact. In addition, the structure of the novel is masterfully inventive; clearly, Conrad was attempting a leap forward in the genre of the novel as he constructed his novel with multiple narratives, striking symbolism, time shifts, and multi-layer characterizations. *Lord Jim*, like many great achievements by many artists, was produced at a time when Conrad was in dire financial straits and was living in a state of great emotional unhappiness.

After *Lord Jim*, Conrad produced one major novel after another – *Nostromo, Typhoon, The Secret Agent, Under Western Eyes, Victory,* and *Chance,* perhaps his most "popular" novel. He was no longer poor, and, ironically, he was no longer as superlatively productive. From 1911 until his death in 1924, he never wrote anything that equaled his early works. His great work was done.

Personally, however, Conrad's life was full. He was recognized widely, and he enjoyed dressing the part of a dandy; it was something he had always enjoyed doing, and now he could financially afford to. He played this role with great enthusiasm. He was a short, tiny man and had a sharp Slavic face which he accentuated with a short beard, and he was playing the "aristocrat," as it were. No one minded, for within literary circles, Conrad was exactly that – a master.

When World War I broke out, Conrad was spending some time in Poland with his wife and sons, and they barely escaped imprisonment. Back in England, Conrad began assembling his entire body of work, which appeared in 1920, and immediately afterward, he was offered a knighthood by the British government. He declined, however, and continued living without national honor, but with immense literary honor instead. He suffered a heart attack in August, 1924, and was buried at Canterbury.

LIST OF CHARACTERS

Lord Jim

A tall, powerfully built young man with piercing blue eyes and a deep voice. On his first assignment at sea, aboard the *Patna,* Jim abandons 800 Moslem pilgrims because he thinks that the ship is going to explode momentarily. Afterward, he is terribly ashamed and unable to live a normal life because he fears that his terrible cowardice will be revealed. It is only after Jim becomes the overseer of a trading post in the far-off Malay Islands that he is able to regain his self-esteem and his sense of honor.

Marlow

A sea captain some twenty years older than Jim. When Marlow first sees Jim, on trial for desertion, he is sure that Jim has a cowardly streak in his nature. Later, however, Marlow begins to identify with Jim, and finally he becomes deeply sympathetic to the sensitive young man. Marlow's final assessment of Jim is that he is "one of us." In other words, we all have one shameful secret in our pasts.

Skipper of the *Patna*

Grossly fat and greasy ("a man cut out of a block of fat"), he embodies evil and cowardice; he is "the incarnation of everything base and vile." It is his voice which Jim hears, seemingly commanding Jim to jump, to abandon the *Patna*.

Egstrom and Blake

Owners of a ship-chandler firm, where Jim is employed as a water-clerk. Egstrom praises Jim's happy energy and honesty, and he is puzzled when he discovers that Jim fled the country because of his overwhelming guilt about the *Patna* incident.

Stein

A wealthy and respected businessman, a naturalist of distinction, and a collector of butterflies and beetles (symbols of sentimentality and romance, and of hard-shelled, unimaginative reality). It is Stein who believes that Jim should *immerse* himself in his romantic nature rather than reject it; therefore, he offers Jim a chance to rebuild his life in far-off Patusan.

Cornelius

Jewel's stepfather; he has mismanaged and bungled Stein's trading operations in Patusan. The buildings and books are in a shambles when Jim arrives to replace him. Cornelius "slinks" and "skulks" around the village, hoping to somehow reestablish himself. He knows that he has failed as a businessman and as a father, and his guilt has soured him on mankind. He foolishly believes that the villainous Brown accepts him as a trusted partner in Brown's plan to loot and destroy Patusan.

Doramin

An enormously fat native chieftain of Patusan. He offers sanctuary to Jim when Jim escapes from Rajah Allang; it is Doramin who kills Jim at the end of the story.

Dain Waris

Doramin's only son; Jim's best friend. He is the first of the Patusan people to believe in Jim's goodness and in his potential as a leader. Dain Waris becomes an innocent victim when Jim naively believes that Brown will leave Patusan peacefully.

Jewel

A white girl who has been raised in Patusan. Jim falls in love with her, and she loves Jim with both fierceness and affection. She is not as trusting of people as Jim is, and she is quick to anger when Jim is threatened. She often guards Jim's door at night. One night in particular, she leads him to a nest of assassins. Ultimately, she cannot forgive Jim for his code of honor, a code which requires his death.

Tamb' Itam

Jim's devoted servant; he saves Jim's life during the assault on Sherif Ali's stockade. It is he who carries Jim's silver ring to Dain Waris as a sign that they can trust Brown to leave Patusan peacefully.

Rajah Allang

A corrupt man who established power over the Patusan natives by force and intimidation. He extorts everything he can from the people and trades it all to foreign buyers. He is awed by Jim's charismatic hold over the natives.

Sherif Ali

A corrupt renegade who lives in the hills and makes frequent raids on the natives. Jim establishes his own sense of power and authority by destroying Sherif Ali's bastion, which hangs over the village like a buzzard's roost.

Brown

Because he once had a respectable background, he calls himself "Gentleman Brown." Now, however, he has become a pirate. By chance, he comes upriver to Patusan, hoping to raid the village for enough food and water to get his pirate crew to Madagascar.

Mr. Denver

Marlow convinces Denver to give Jim a job at his rice mill. All goes well until one of the *Patna's* crew turns up at the mill and tries to blackmail Jim. Not knowing why Jim flees the mill, Denver writes an angry letter to Marlow.

The French Lieutenant

He boards the *Patna* the morning after she is abandoned, and he remains on board until she is towed to port. The trip was disappointing, he says, because there was no wine available for dinner. Talking to Marlow, he reveals that he is cynical about the nature of bravery.

Chester

An Australian adventurer, he believes that he has found an uncharted island so rich in guano (bird droppings) that he will soon be rich beyond measure. He unsuccessfully pleads with Marlow to convince Jim that he can find a new and satisfying life for himself as an overseer on the guano island.

Brierly

To all appearances, he has led a model life as a seaman; his future seems full of promise. Brierly presides as judge at Jim's trial for deserting the *Patna*, and as the trial progresses, he so closely identifies with Jim that he begins to fear that someday he too might commit an error similar to Jim's jumping from the *Patna*. Therefore, he sets his affairs in order and commits suicide by "jumping" into the sea.

The Dane

A cross-eyed lieutenant in the Royal Siamese Navy who insults Jim while they are playing billiards. Jim tosses him into the sea.

BRIEF PLOT SYNOPSIS

We are introduced to Jim (later, Lord Jim) at a time when he was working as a water-clerk for a ship-chandler firm in the Far East. It was menial work, but Jim seemed fairly happy, and everyone liked him. They knew him simply as "Jim." Yet, as the plot unfolds, with Conrad's skillful analysis of Jim's character, we gradually realize that Jim was not "merely" Jim; he was "one of us."

Jim was born and raised in an English parson's home, and when he was still a young lad, he decided to make the sea his career; thus, he enrolled on a training ship for officers of the merchant marine. He did well and advanced to third place in navigation. While still aboard the training ship, he met his first test of courage.

But during that test of courage, Jim held back in fear when he was called upon to assist a vessel injured in a fierce storm. Afterward, he justified himself and rationalized that he was not really afraid; he was simply waiting for a challenge that would be equal to his heroism. Next time, he would be heroic. He was convinced that he would have another chance.

Some time later, an injury from a falling spar put Jim in the hospital, and after recovering, he shipped out as first mate on the *Patna,* an old iron tramp steamer bound for holy places with 800 Moslem religious pilgrims. The other four officers of the *Patna* were riff-raff. Accordingly, Jim held himself aloof from them.

On a calm, dark night in the Arabian Sea, the *Patna* ran over some floating wreckage and got badly damaged in her forepeak compartment. Jim discovered the damage and saw that the sea was pressing in on the bulkhead, which walled in the hold, where hundreds of the pilgrims were asleep. The bulkhead bulged. It could not possibly withstand the pressure. Jim was convinced that within minutes the sea would rush in and the pilgrims would all be drowned. With too few lifeboats and no time, there was no possible salvation for everybody on board.

Meanwhile, the skipper and the other officers struggled to lower a lifeboat. Jim despised their cowardice and refused to help them. Then he spotted a squall bearing down on the *Patna*, and he knew that the lightest shudder would burst the bulkhead. It might be a matter of seconds.

The officers got the boat over the side, while the squall closed in with dark, tumbling clouds. The first gust of wind hit the *Patna*, and she plunged. Jim was sure that it was her last tremor. He jumped.

Hours of horror followed. The other officers resented Jim's presence in the lifeboat. They watched as the lights of the *Patna* seemed to go out, and meanwhile, Jim listened and seemed to hear the hysterical screams of the helpless passengers. Once, he even considered throwing himself over the lifeboat and swimming back.

Before sundown of the following day, the ship *Avondale* picked up the four men, and ten days later, it delivered them to an Eastern port.

The story which the *Patna's* skipper invented as their alibi for desertion was immediately useless when they heard the news that a French man-o-war had discovered the *Patna* listing badly, deserted by her officers, and towed it into Aden.

At this news, the skipper vanished, and the two engineers drank themselves into a hospital. Jim faced the official inquiry panel alone. He defended himself doggedly and insisted that there hadn't been a chance in a million that the *Patna* could have survived. "There was not the thickness of a sheet of paper between the right and wrong of this affair."

At the inquiry, a man named Marlow entered the scene, and throughout most of the novel, the reader will see Jim through Marlow's sympathetic eyes and emotions.

Deeply interested in the young, wholesome-looking Englishman who seemed so "doomed," Marlow attended the inquiry and tried to discover why Jim deserted the *Patna*.

Then, a strange and dramatic circumstance brought Marlow and Jim together. Jim confronted Marlow and accused him of calling him a "wretched cur." Marlow convinced Jim that another person had made the remark and was referring not to Jim, but to an actual dog. Jim realized that he had exposed his low opinion of himself to Marlow.

Nevertheless, Marlow found himself even more drawn to Jim, and so he invited the young man to have dinner with him at Malabar House. There, Jim related the story of what happened that night aboard the *Patna*. Marlow was puzzled by the young man's attitude toward himself, and, despite himself, he caught glimpses of his own tormented soul within Jim.

The inquiry ended, Jim lost his naval certificate, and Marlow invited him to his hotel room, where the reader sees the agony of the promising young officer who now regarded himself as "no better than a vagabond."

Marlow found a job for Jim, and the young man did well and pleased his employer. But suddenly, Jim disappeared. Someone had mentioned the *Patna* affair and Jim could not endure it. Under such circumstances, Jim left job after job until every waterfront character throughout the Orient knew Jim's story.

Marlow finally confided Jim's story to a Herr Stein, a philosophical old trader with a fabulous butterfly collection. Stein, who had never seen Jim, labeled him a "romantic" and suggested that Jim go to Patusan, an isolated island community in a Malay state where three warring factions were contending for supremacy. In Patusan, Stein had an unprofitable trading post under the direction of a slimy Portuguese, Cornelius. Jim could take over the trading post and begin a new life; no one would know him in Patusan.

Stein's offer delighted Jim. He felt that he could now bury his past completely and no one would ever find out about it. Stein also gave Jim a silver ring, a symbol of eternal friendship between Stein and Doramin, chief of the Bugis Malays in Patusan.

Alone, Jim traveled upriver to Patusan, but he was soon captured by Rajah Allang's men. He did, however, manage to leap over the stockade and escape to Doramin's village, where he showed him Stein's silver ring, symbolic of eternal friendship between Stein and Doramin. Afterward, Jim was warmly welcomed and was protected.

Jim's hopes seemed about to be realized. Doramin's son, Dain Waris, was a strong, intelligent youth about Jim's age, and the two worked together to put down the vandalism of Sherif Ali and to bring Rajah Allang under control.

Jim felt secure in the love and trust of all the Malays. He had a noble and beloved friend in Dain Waris, and he fell in love with a girl, Jewel, who shared his life.

After two years, Marlow visited Jim at Patusan, but it wasn't a completely successful visit; Marlow felt that even his temporary intrusion into this idyllic existence upset Jim and those who were close to him. He resolved never again to visit Patusan.

The outside world also reentered Jim's sanctuary in the person of "Gentleman Brown," a renegade Australian who stole a ship and, with a band of desperate seamen, traveled upriver to Patusan. He intended to plunder the settlement and supply his ship for a voyage to Madagascar.

When the bandits arrived, Jim was away, but the village people under Dain Waris repulsed the invaders and drove them to a knoll, where the white men were able to throw up a temporary defense.

When Jim returned, Doramin, Dain Waris, and all of the villagers urged immediate annihilation for the robbers, but Jim decided to talk to Brown.

Brown did not really know anything about Jim's past, but he knew enough of his own vile history, and so he judged Jim by himself; thus, Jim's old fears and shame returned. Brown was able to see that Jim had a guilty conscience about something.

Jim did not want bloodshed, so he promised Brown and his men safe conduct down the river. Then he made a persuasive speech to the Bugis in which he pledged his own life as security – should any harm come to any of the villagers as a result of his letting Brown's party go free.

Brown, advised and guided by the slimy Cornelius, left as planned, but he treacherously ambushed a party of Malays under Dain Waris on the way downriver. The chief's son and many of his soldiers were killed.

Survivors brought Dain Waris' body to his father, Doramin. On the young man's hand was the silver ring which Jim had sent to him as a pledge of Brown's good faith. Someone took the ring and held it up for Doramin to see. The old chief let out "one fierce cry, deep from the chest, a cry of pain and fury."

Meanwhile, the awful news reached Jim. His new life had fallen into ruins. The Malays would never again trust him. He had three choices. He could run; he could fight (he had an arsenal); or he could give himself up according to Malay custom. Jewel and Tamb' Itam, Jim's servant, urged him to fight or, at least, flee, but Jim deliberately crossed the creek and climbed the hill to Doramin's village. Stooping down, he lifted the sheet from Dain Waris' face. Then, alone and unarmed, he faced Doramin.

As the old chief rose up, the silver ring fell from his lap and rolled to Jim's feet. Doramin shot Jim through the chest, and as he did so, Lord Jim flashed a proud and unflinching look toward all of the assembled Malays. Then he fell at Doramin's feet, a hero in death.

SUMMARIES AND COMMENTARIES

CHAPTER 1

Summary

Jim was an impressive young man – about six feet tall and powerfully built – extremely intense, self-assertive, and always dressed in spotless white. He was a popular and successful water-clerk – that is, he competed against all the other water-clerks in port to be the very first man to greet a newly docked sea captain and steer him to a vast supply store (a "ship's chandler") filled with all the items that a ship would need for its next voyage. While the ship remained docked, Jim had to court, cajole, and serve the captain as a loyal friend and as a patient, good-natured companion so that the captain would spend a great deal of money at the ship-chandler's.

Jim always drew good wages, but he never stayed at one port for very long; he had "something of the unknown" about him, something that set him apart, something which Conrad calls "an exquisite sensibility."

We are also told that for many years, Jim went by only one name – Jim – because he wanted to hide a "fact" about himself and when that "fact" surfaced in seaport gossip, Jim would leave town very suddenly, always traveling "farther east," toward the rising sun.

It was while Jim was working among the Malays (the Bugis) that he acquired the other half of the name by which men would know him. The natives dubbed him "Tuan Jim," or Lord Jim.

Seemingly, Jim became interested in sailing and adventure as a young boy, because one day, after reading some "light holiday literature," presumably about sailing, he immediately decided that the sea would be his vocation. Not long afterward, he was sent to a "training-ship for officers." He was generally well-liked at the school; he was cool-headed, clever, and had an enviable physique. His job stationed him at the ship's fore-top, from which he could scan the surroundings and look down at the other boys, as if from a very privileged distance. From his high post, Jim daydreamed that he was being readied for a heroic "role"; he romantically envisioned himself rescuing people from hurricanes and then surviving half-naked on a deserted island. He saw himself quelling tempers and putting down inflamed mutinies. In his dreams, he was always the essence of fidelity and duty.

One winter's day at dusk, Jim heard a call to help a coaster which had crashed into a schooner. He stopped and held his breath in awe while the other boys clamored over the rails and were lowered away. Jim was half-ready to leap overboard when the captain unexpectedly gripped his shoulder. "Too late, youngster," he said. "Better luck next time."

Later the other boys, particularly one boy with "a face like a girl's," loudly celebrated their successful rescue of the victims of the collision. The pretty young boy – and not Jim – was the hero of the evening. Jim pondered over his failure to act, his hesitating too long. Why hadn't he acted? Next time, he vowed to himself, he would act faster and better than anyone, but this time, why should he have risked life and limb for such a trivial "rescue effort"? He breathed deeply, eager for a new challenge that would be worthy of him.

Commentary

Our first view of Lord Jim, the protagonist of the novel, is that of a dedicated and moral person; consequently, we are immediately aware that this novel will deal with moral and ethical issues.

Many critics refer to this novel as an "impressionistic" novel because we are given the impression of a man who, at three critical times in his life, is faced with a difficult choice, and, each time, he chooses incorrectly. First, he must choose whether, as a cadet, he will join in rescuing a sinking ship; he doesn't. Second, he must choose whether or not to jump from the sinking *Patna,* leaving 800 pilgrims to drown; he jumps. Third, he must choose whether or not to have Gentleman Brown killed; he chooses not to. In each case, because of his romantic illusions, Lord Jim makes the wrong decision and we see how these wrong decisions affect him.

Throughout this novel, we are constantly reminded that Jim is "one of us" – that what Lord Jim does is probably what most of us would do under the same circumstances, and until we are confronted with a similar situation, we do not know whether or not we also would "jump." As the critic Albert Guerard states, "The universality of Lord Jim is even more obvious, since nearly everyone has jumped off some *Patna* and most of us have been compelled to live on, desperately or quietly engaged in reconciling what we are with what we would like to be."

The first four chapters of the novel offer a view of Jim from the omniscient author's (Conrad's) point-of-view. The rest of the novel presents views of Jim from Marlow's point-of-view, as well as additional points-of-view from Jim's father's letter, from documents, and from Gentleman Brown's account of Jim.

Significantly, also, these first four chapters show us Jim's early life and the influence of "light holiday reading" on him, his heroic dreams, a key incident in his sea training, his accident, the voyage of the *Patna* up until the moment when the ship strikes a submerged wreck, and a portion of the courtroom scene where the accused is being questioned.

In Chapter 1, we are given a physical description of Jim; he is an ideal specimen of humanity – tall, handsome, powerfully built, clean cut, and apparently popular. Then Conrad offers us the first incongruity – Jim, as a water-clerk for a ship-chandler, is outstanding in this position (and others) until unexpectedly "he would throw up the job and depart." Likewise, if anyone found out his last name, he would leave immediately. Already, then, Conrad lets us know that there is "something unknown" about Jim's past which caused him to act mysteriously and erratically.

Later, Jim will be seen, by Stein and others, as a romantic, and Conrad lets us know that Jim's love of the sea was a result of "light holiday reading." Even in training, Jim tried to see "himself saving people from sinking ships. . . . in a hurricane swimming through a surf," and performing all sorts of heroic and romantic deeds, living more in the world of fantasy than in reality.

Reality intruded into Jim's dreams, however, when he failed his first test of courage. All the other cadets rushed to the aid of a sinking ship, but Jim remained aboard ship – almost paralyzed. Too late, he tried to join the others. After the others returned, Jim fantasized that next time he would perform greater feats of heroism. Thus, Jim failed his first test and resorted again to dreaming about acts of courage.

CHAPTER 2

Summary

After two years of naval training, Jim's dreams of romance seemingly became reality. While still a young man, he was assigned to be the chief mate of a fine ship, but it was soon apparent that his new job was both monotonous and barren. Yet, curiously, Jim was addicted, "enslaved," as it were, to life at sea. Jim loved the sea because he felt constantly challenged by its savage capriciousness. He felt that at any time, he could triumph over its untamed power. Ironically, he had never been tested by the sea; only once, in fact, had he glimpsed the sea's "sinister something," that power which reveals that the sea can, if it chooses, smash, destroy, and annihilate everything, including Jim's individual and unique life.

During the single time that Jim witnessed the deadly fury of the sea, he was wounded. A heavy spar from the ship's mast fell on him from high up. As he lay on his back, he felt pleased that he didn't have to be on deck during the storm. Then he was swept with guilt.

When fine weather returned, Jim was taken to a hospital in Singapore. His recovery was slow, and his ship sailed without him. At first, Jim was wary and disdainful of Singapore's "bewitching breath" which seemed to smell of softness and decay. And yet Jim was increasingly fascinated by the white men whom he saw. He realized that unlike the heroic figures of his romantic dreams, these men "did well" on a very small allowance of danger and work.

Suddenly, he decided *not* to go home. He accepted the position of chief mate on the *Patna*, an old, rusty steamer which was owned by a Chinese, chartered by an Arab, and captained by a "blood-and-iron" German, steering toward various holy places with 800 ragged, hopeful, and meek Moslem pilgrims crowded into every crevice and cranny.

Commentary

The actual day-to-day routine of being first mate was "strangely barren" and dully monotonous; it contrasted significantly with Jim's romantic dreams and fantasies. Jim's injury served merely to place him in a hospital in an "Eastern port" (most probably Singapore) where he was in danger of "lounging through the days in easy chairs . . .

with eternal serenity." Thus, he determined to take the first available passage out and, consequently, he signed on as first mate on the *Patna*, a rusty, old dilapidated steamer, "eaten with rust worse than a condemned water-tank." It was commanded by an incompetent, disreputable captain and a crew from which Jim stood out; he was too "perfect." Conrad's description of the ship and the captain portends that this ship is unsafe and that an unfortunate incident is imminent.

Reading the description of the pilgrims boarding the ship, one is reminded of cattle being blindly herded and crowded into small, unclean quarters. The German captain's view of the pilgrims as "cattle" emphasizes his disgust with them and justifies, in his mind, his later desertion of them to seemingly certain death – a view that completely separates him from Jim, who is deeply and profoundly affected by his actions. Jim's jumping from the *Patna* controls the rest of his life.

Concerning the episode of the *Patna* and the pilgrims, Conrad is basing this part of *Lord Jim* upon an actual event. The actual ship was named the *Jeddah,* and it was loaded with about 1,000 pilgrims. When it almost foundered, the ship was abandoned by the captain and the crew, who were picked up by a steamship and taken to the port of Aden, where they reported the "loss" of their ship. The next day, the *Jeddah* was towed into the port of Aden with all of her pilgrim/passengers still on board. This was a naval scandal, and the disgrace became widely known throughout the nautical world, causing horrendous gossip and a full inquiry. But Conrad's readers will not be informed about the events concerning the *Patna* until later, and even then, the facts will be only slowly revealed.

CHAPTER 3

Summary

The stillness of the night and the serenity of the stars seemed to shed an assurance of everlasting security, and the *Patna,* moving smoothly and routinely across the Arabian Sea, seemd to be a perfect part of a safe universe.

On deck, Jim paced during his night watch. As usual, he was dreaming, his imagination lulled by romantic visions of courageous deeds and bold action. He had a full and wonderful sense of self-confidence.

Minutes before he was relieved, he saw the pig-like outline of the skipper come up on deck; he was repulsed by the man's disgustingly naked belly, glistening and obscene with greasy sweat. The second engineer also came up, and he began to argue drunkenly with the skipper.

Then suddenly, everything changed. The gesturing engineer, descending below the deck, lurched violently and pitched head-down, cursing loudly. Jim and the skipper staggered forward. Distant thunder rumbled, then there was silence. The ship quivered, then regained its slow, peaceful progress.

Commentary

This chapter devotes itself to presenting a repulsive picture of Jim's captain and fellow officers. The captain, the chief engineer, and the second engineer are all described in derogatory terms in order to foreshadow their despicable, disreputable, horrible immoral actions – that is, the desertion of the 800 Moslem pilgrims to certain death.

For example, the immoral nature of the captain is first expressed in his physical description – "There was something obscene in . . . his naked flesh . . . [his] odious and fleshly figure . . . fixed itself in his memory as the incarnation of everything vile and base that lurked in the world we love." In addition to the captain's obesity is the drunkenness of the second engineer. Against these people, Jim and his romantic purity and ideals stand in sharp relief. And yet in the crucial moment, as we later learn, Jim "jumps" along with these immoral derelicts.

Later in the novel, and especially at the end of Chapter 3, note Conrad's technique of impressionistically suggesting that "something" has happened. Conrad, however, will not reveal fully "the jump" until quite later. In fact, the reader should try to determine at what point in this novel it becomes perfectly clear that Jim did indeed "jump" and abandon the *Patna* and the Moslem pilgrims.

CHAPTER 4

Summary

The narrative resumes a month or so later, and we are now in the police court of an Eastern port. An official hearing was called to investigate "the *Patna* incident" in an attempt to determine what struck the ship and what happened on board after the mysterious collision that night.

Standing in a box above the hot, packed courtroom, Jim was the only white member of the *Patna's* crew to answer to the panel of inquiry. His answers were obviously painful and difficult, and he shivered, his mind flying.

Slowly, in fragments and half-statements of memory, Jim explained to the panel that he tried to determine that night if any damage had been done to the ship; he remembered that he immediately realized that the hatch in the front of the ship was rapidly filling with water. Clearly, there was a hole in the bottom of the ship. Only one wall kept the ship from being flooded, and if that wall broke, they were doomed. In shock, yet strangely calm, he went to warn the captain, and he met the second engineer, who was complaining about a broken arm. Jim explained what had happened, and the engineer dashed toward the captain, shouting and swearing in panic. The captain silenced him and sent him below to shut off the hot engines before the icy water broke against them.

Lost in futility and frustration and wiping his damp forehead, Jim unexpectedly saw a "distinctive looking" white man in the room, sitting apart. His face was worn and clouded, but his eyes were "straight, interested, and clear." Jim had seen this man before—he was sure of it—and this man seemed "to be aware of [Jim's] hopeless difficulty."

Commentary

This chapter shifts to some time later. Here, the reader could be justifiably confused about the time, the place, the purpose of the "inquiry," and the indistinct introduction of a strange man called Marlow.

Throughout these first four chapters, we see Jim through the omniscient narrator as a magnificent physical specimen endowed with an "exquisite sensibility," a man who dreams of "valorous deeds" and who lives on an idealistic level. Later, we will realize that this view is ironic: here, for example, Jim is on trial at a court of inquiry, and he is filled with horror and shame, and yet we don't know the reason why. Jim is forced, we hear, to give facts—even though facts do not answer the essential questions: "They wanted facts. Facts. They demanded facts of him, as if facts could explain anything."

Meantime, Jim knew that "only a meticulous precision of statement would bring out the true horror behind the appalling face of things." Jim's realizations, by the very nature of the language, imply that something horrible has happened, yet the reader is still essentially in the dark as to the nature of Jim's "horror" and his "shame."

In summary, the first four chapters have presented, from an omniscient view, (1) Jim's early life and training for the sea, (2) his dreams of performing acts of courage and heroism, (3) an important chance to be a hero during his sea training, (4) the voyage on the *Patna* until some unexplained misfortune strikes, and (5) Jim's being tried for some unknown but horrible and shameful act.

CHAPTER 5

Summary

After dinner, while talking to some guests, Marlow recalls more details about the much-discussed "*Patna* incident." It was his "guardian devil," he says, that caused him to have such a keen interest in the inquiry.

It seems that four officers deserted the *Patna* when they believed it to be sinking, leaving the rest of the crew and the 800 Moslem pilgrims to be cooked alive in the hot steam of the sinking ship, leaving them as though they were "only natives." The *Patna*, however, did not explode and sink; it arrived safely at Aden, a port on the Red Sea, and now its officers had to stand trial for deserting their ship.

Only Jim, however, was available to testify. After the obese captain received a tongue-lashing from the Harbour Master, he squeezed his soft, massive bulk into a tiny carriage and vanished. Marlow talked to the two engineers who were hospitalized, but he was unable to discover any relevant information about the affair. The first engineer swore that there were thousands of pink toads under his hospital bed, and the second engineer swore that the *Patna* did indeed sink and that it was full of reptiles.

Ultimately, it was not Jim's "crime" that interested and disturbed Marlow; it was Jim's weakness, for despite Jim's cowardly flaw, and despite the fact that he deserted the *Patna*, Marlow admits that he himself would have "trusted the deck" to Jim "on the strength of a single glance." And yet, "it wouldn't have been safe."

Commentary

The end of Chapter 4 mentioned an observer named Marlow who was present at Jim's trial, and now that Jim is placed before us as a man on trial, we must begin, through Marlow's eyes, to make judgments about Jim. Marlow will now select and objectify our views of Jim.

Marlow is theoretically telling the story to some unnamed listeners (one of them, we know, is named Charley), and many readers have questioned this device – that is, in Conrad's "Author's Note," he writes that critics have "argued that no man could have been expected to talk all that time, and other men to listen so long." Conrad answered the objection by saying that, first, some members of Parliament speak for six hours in Parliament without stopping and that, second, Jim's story is so intriguing that it would hold the attention of the listeners.

Chapter 5, however, still does not enlighten the reader as to the true nature of the *Patna* episode. Rather, Conrad focuses on the four officers from Marlow's point-of-view: the captain is presented as "the fattest man in the whole blessed tropical belt" and is elephantine in nature and thoroughly obscene and disgusting in every way. The other three men are all contrasts to the captain. The chief engineer and the second engineer are almost insignificant, and in total contrast to all of them is Jim – the magnificent, broad-shouldered youth whose very appearance seems to inspire confidence.

Most important, however, is the fact that Marlow realized that Jim is "one of us." This phrase, as noted earlier, will become one of the principal themes of the novel. That is, if Jim is "one of us," then any of us readers, finding ourselves in the same predicament as Jim found himself, would probably react exactly as Jim did. Therefore, throughout the novel we should gauge Jim's actions against how we ourselves might likely act in a similar situation.

But, as yet, as noted above, we still do not know what the horrible, shameful, disgraceful action was that Jim committed; we know only that everyone reacted violently and with deep resentment and indignation.

Marlow prepares us for Jim's remaining all alone in port to testify by emphasizing in great detail how the captain suddenly "departed, disappeared, vanished, absconded." The second engineer is also dispensed with, and the chief engineer drank himself into such a coma that he couldn't testify. These drastic actions intrigue the reader as to the nature of the forthcoming testimony.

CHAPTER 6

Summary

Marlow now tells the dinner guests more about Jim's trial before the panel of inquiry. The trial, he says, became something of a public "event." Here was a handsome young man on trial for leaving almost a thousand poor and ragged religious pilgrims to almost certain death. Justice demanded punishment, and Jim, almost willingly it seemed, faced his judges alone and endured the grueling and exhausting inquisition. The trial, Marlow says, was ultimately unsatisfactory because it was an exercise in futility. Instead of trying to determine the philosophical why's of Jim's behavior, the inquiry focused entirely upon the factual and pragmatic how's of the affair.

At the end of the second day of Jim's trial, Marlow remembers that a very revealing incident occurred. An ugly, mangy dog was weaving in and out of the crowd, and a man laughed aloud, remarking, "Look at that wretched cur."

Instantaneously, Jim whirled and accused Marlow of calling him a cur, and it was only with great difficulty that Marlow was able to convince Jim that it was another man who had spoken and that he had referred to an actual dog.

Afterward, Jim was terribly humiliated. His face turned crimson, the clear blue of his eyes darkened, and he seemed to be on the verge of tears. For that single moment, Marlow says, he witnessed how "a single word had stripped [Jim] of his discretion." All of Jim's almost successfully disguised suffering during the trial surfaced; without meaning to, Jim had revealed an explosive, volatile side of his nature.

Jim turned away instantly, frightened to have revealed himself so nakedly, but Marlow was so thoroughly captivated by the young man that he followed him and invited him to dinner.

Commentary

The inexplicability of human action is presented through the story of Captain Brierly. Here we have a man who has risen to the pinnacle of his profession by the age of thirty-two, has never made a mistake, nor had an accident or mishap. He has no debts, no entanglements, and yet, for no seeming reason, he goes about logically and systematically putting his ship into the hands of the chief mate, Mr. Jones, and then he commits suicide by diving into the sea with iron ballasts fastened to his body.

Ultimately Jim's actions, however, will seem as inexplicable as Captain Brierly's. Some critics even believe that the captain is so troubled by the actions of someone like Jim, who is such an outstanding gentleman . . . "one of us," that the analogy troubles Brierly too much; therefore, he calmly prepares his own suicide so that he won't have to live with the knowledge that he too might someday do the exact same thing.

Of course, it is also very significant that Brierly wants to furnish sufficient money (200 rupees) for Jim to disappear because the entire trial and inquiry and the "infernal publicity is too shocking"; by analogy, the trial is a reflection upon a fellow Englishman in an alien land.

Again, by the end of Chapter 6, Conrad has still not revealed Jim's full, actual predicament, and Brierly intrigues us further by asking, "Why are we tormenting that young chap?" We don't know; we are still in the dark as to the nature of Jim's torment.

Marlow's first meeting with Jim is charged with emotion as Jim mistakenly thinks that Marlow has referred to him as a "wretched cur." By the time the mistake is corrected, Marlow is able to persuade Jim to have dinner with him, and we now anticipate hearing more of Jim's story.

CHAPTER 7

Summary

During dinner, the wine loosened Jim's tongue, and he began his painful story. Now, he has no money, no job, no future as a sailor, and he has shamed his pastor father, who is incapable of understanding what has happened. Impulsively, Jim asks Marlow if he can understand it all. What would Marlow have done?

Jim said that after he and his fellow officers were picked up and taken ashore, he learned that the *Patna* did not sink. The news seemed impossible to believe; the *Patna* had been doomed. Jim recalled in detail how he himself examined the bulkhead of the ship; he remembered how it had bulged, ready to crack momentarily. There were seven lifeboats and 800 passengers. If Jim had alerted the passengers, their panic would have caused virtual chaos. He was surrounded by a sea ready to swallow him up, and he was surrounded by 800 sleeping natives who would soon be drowning, screaming like frightened, panicking animals. "They were dead. Nothing could save them!"

Jim swore to Marlow that he was not afraid of death, even as they were talking; nor was he afraid of death then, and Marlow was inclined to believe him—simply because Jim's mind dwelled not on death, but on his fear of unleashed panic. Marlow realized also that Jim never tried to suggest that what the crewmen did was not terribly wrong, and "therein lies his distinction."

In anguish, Jim moaned, "What a chance missed!" What should he have done? Even now, he didn't know. All he could do was remember what he did do.

Commentary

Chapter 7 allows the reader to know more about Jim's predicament, but not before Marlow again lets us know that Jim "was of the right sort; he was one of us." The repetition of this phrase functions to remind us again and again that we are like Jim and would probably have reacted the same way that he did, especially since Jim states his case directly to Marlow in such a way that aligns all of us to Jim. "Do you know what you would have done? Do you? and you don't think yourself . . . you don't think yourself a—a—cur?"

When Jim maintains that after this terrible event, "this . . . hell," he can never go home again, and after he explains further that with his "certificate gone, career broken, no money . . . no work that he could obtain," that he is, in essence, ruined, the reader's interest in Jim's disgrace is intensified.

The reason for the narrative of Jim's exploits lies simply in his statement to Marlow: "It is all in being ready. I wasn't; not—not then. I don't want to excuse myself, but I would like to explain—I would like somebody to understand—somebody—one person at least! You! Why not you?" Thus Marlow, through his initial empathy for this young and handsome man, is chosen by him to be the recipient of this horrible experience.

Our first real intimation as to what really happened comes when Marlow says: "So that bulkhead held out after all," and then a second hint comes when Jim murmurs: "Ah! What a chance missed! My God! what a chance missed."

It is then after some contemplation that Marlow finally reacts and says, "If you had stuck to the ship, you mean." Still, even the most sensitive readers might miss this clue or not come to the full implication of its meaning. For many readers, it will not be clear what happened until much later, when we hear that the *Patna* was towed to Aden. Some readers, of course, will not be fully aware of what has happened until they hear the French lieutenant's story. But nevertheless, most readers, by now, are forming some definite impressions about the character of Jim and the character of Marlow, as well as some of the other characters.

When Jim maintains that there was nothing that he could do for the pilgrims ("They were dead! Nothing could save them! There weren't boats enough for half of them, but there was not time! No time! No time!"), he also protests that he was not thinking of saving himself, that he was not afraid of death.

At this point, Marlow interprets for the reader by saying that Jim "was not afraid of death, but . . . he was afraid of the emergency." Marlow then interprets for us that Jim "might have been resigned to die, but I suspect he wanted to die without added terrors, quietly, in a sort of peaceful trance." Marlow will continue to interpret for the reader, but we should always remember that we are still free to disagree with his viewpoint.

CHAPTER 8

Summary

Marlow now recounts more of what Jim told him. On that fateful night, Jim could recall that he was running along the deck, stepping with difficulty over the sleeping Moslems. One man asked for water, and Jim hit him, then thrust his own water bottle at him. Later, on the bridge, Jim again felt alone and doomed. He stood frozen, unable to decide what action to take. He was not afraid to die, but he was paralyzed by the possibility of his dying anonymously among hundreds of screaming natives, disappearing forever beneath the exploding ship.

Marlow admits that had he been aboard ship, he probably would not have "given a counterfeit farthing" for the possibility that the *Patna* would not sink. Then he recalls that as he was listening to Jim, he realized that Jim was not speaking to him as a person, but as a symbol – someone who would justify what Jim had done, as though Marlow were "an inseparable partner . . . another possessor of his soul." For Marlow, this was additional proof that Jim was "one of us."

Marlow reminded Jim that a man couldn't continually "be prepared" for any and all preconceived emergencies. It was the unexpected which always happened, Marlow told him, never what one expected to happen. Jim scoffed and began to sulk. The *Patna*, his fellow officers, and even the sea had tricked him. It had all been a cruel, unfair, and tragic joke.

Then Jim returned to the events that happened the night he deserted the *Patna*. One of the officers, he said, pleaded with him to help free a lifeboat, but he refused, and later he slugged the officer. Then the officer shouted out that Jim was a coward. Remembering that moment, Jim laughed with such a savage bitterness that the hotel guests stopped talking and turned to look at Jim in bewilderment.

Commentary

Chapter 8 continues in an indirect manner, further unraveling the mysterious catastrophe connected with the *Patna*. Conrad, through Marlow, continues to approach the incident indirectly (by circumlocution). For example, instead of attacking the narrative directly, he gives us the reactions of the various members of the crew.

He examines Jim first because as first mate, Jim has all of the lifeboats ready for use in spite of the fact that there are not enough to save even half of the pilgrims. Then we see Jim panicking when one of the pilgrims asks for some drinking water for his sick child; Jim interprets the request as a threat and reacts with hostility.

Further panicking is seen when Jim feels a "heavy blow on [his] shoulder" only to discover that it is the second engineer, and the captain himself charges against Jim until he realizes that it is actually Jim. Then Jim hears the captain say that he is going to "clear out" – a horribly shocking statement. Throughout this narration, Conrad (Marlow) is conveying the confusion and horror of the situation which creates the panic and confusion, causing Jim to jump without ever really knowing why he jumped.

Again in this chapter, Marlow and the reader are reinvolved in the mystery when Jim once again cries out: "You think me a cur for standing there, but what would you have done? What! You can't tell – nobody can tell." And then in the very next paragraph, Marlow reinforces this idea and again repeats it: "The occasion was obscure, insignificant – what you will: a lost youngster, one of a million – but then he was one of us," and thus each of us might have done exactly as Jim did.

Later in the novel, Stein will categorize Jim as being an extreme romantic. Here in this chapter, Conrad is already preparing us for this scene as he emphasizes Jim's simplicity and his innocence – two qualities most often associated with the romantic.

It is Jim's innocence which makes it so hard for him to deal with the deviousness of the other members of the crew, especially when the first engineer attacks Jim and then cries out: "Won't you save your own life – you infernal coward?" Jim cannot react to this except to laugh bitterly over the irony of it, especially now that he has been internationally branded as a coward because he did save his life by jumping.

Even though the reader is still not informed precisely as to the true nature of the *Patna* episode, this chapter does provide a final clue: "And still she floated! These sleeping pilgrims were destined to accomplish their whole pilgrimage to the bitterness of some other end." By now there should be enough clues for the reader to form a very definite view – that the crew, thinking that the ship would sink, abandoned the ship and yet the ship miraculously did *not* sink.

CHAPTER 9

Summary

Watching the other officers battle to free the lifeboats, Jim was so maddened by the sudden "black, black" squall and the impending disaster that he grabbed his knife and sliced the ropes holding the lifeboats; then he gazed on the almost comical struggling scene below "of four men fighting like mad with a stubborn lifeboat." All their efforts were futile. He hated these insect-like men. He told Marlow that had he, Marlow, been on board, he too "would have leaped" overboard, as Jim did when he heard the captain yelling from a lifeboat to jump!

Jim recalled the black rain squall that "sneaked up" and loomed overhead, eating up "a third of the sky" before it broke over the ship and began to awaken the Moslems. The threat of drowning during a furious storm from heaven, lost among a frenzied mob of screaming natives, filled Jim with such alarm that it seemed as though life itself were pounding against him, beating on him "like the sea upon a rock."

It was pitch black. Jim could not see. He could hear only the skipper and an engineer yelling for a comrade who died suddenly of a heart attack. The *Patna* seemed to slip, then go into a slow, downward plunge – and at that moment, Jim jumped. He jumped without thought and without realizing that he had jumped. He no longer felt as if he were in control of his actions. Something else – something larger and more powerful than he – was now controlling him; all that he could do was passively accept the unknown. He felt that he was a hopeless victim, lost at the bottom "of an everlasting deep hole."

Commentary

Chapter 9 finally presents Jim's jump from the presumably sinking ship. But the jump is surrounded by so many real and so many impressionistic details that it is difficult to separate the real from the impressionistic. From a distance, Jim wants to laugh at the tragic-comic frantic actions of the captain and the crew: "It was funny enough to make angels weep." Then suddenly a squall came up and the crew was sure that the squall would immediately sink the ship: "In absolute stillness there was some chance for the ship to keep afloat a few minutes longer, [but] the least disturbance of the sea would make an end of her instantly." At this, the others "displayed their extreme aversion to die."

Jim soon realizes "that there was nothing in common between him and these men," and when Jim expresses his anger at them for their cowardly actions, the entire crew here (and later) turns against him, calling him a fool and pointing out that he wouldn't have a ghost of a chance if they awaken "that lot of brutes [the pilgrims]. . . . They will batter your head for you."

Consequently, after the captain and the crew are safely in the water, they call for George, the third engineer (who, unknown to them, is dead from a heart attack) to jump into the lifeboat, but they do not call for Jim to jump. And later, Jim's life is endangered by the hatred of these cowards.

Amidst the confusion, the oncoming squall, the definite sensation of the ship sinking, the terrified and desperate activities of the captain and the crew, and the sudden dipping of the bow of the ship, Jim is completely lost in confusion. Again he aligns Marlow and the readers by asking "What would you have done? You are sure of yourself – aren't you? What would you do if you felt now – this minute – the house here move, just move a little under your chair? Leap! By heavens! you would take one spring from where you sit and land in that clump of bushes yonder."

The answer, of course, is that almost every one of us, amid such confusion and confronted with certain death, would also have jumped. Even Marlow admits how uncomfortable it made him feel, and he was careful not to answer because of his fear of being "drawn into a fatal admission about myself." And furthermore, Marlow reiterates that "really he [Jim] was too much like one of us . . ."

Thus, amidst all the confusion, with the captain and the crew calling for George (the dead third engineer) to jump, and with Jim feeling that the ship "was going down, down, head first under me . . ." he apparently jumped. Jim puts his actions in the past: "I had jumped . . . it seems." He doesn't actually remember the jump, only the painful landing in the boat and then he feels regretfully that he "had jumped into a well – into an everlasting deep hole." The rest of his life will hereafter be determined by this one act, and later, his every job and his every act until, finally, his tragic decision concerning Gentleman Brown will be determined by this tragic jump.

CHAPTERS 10 & 11

Summary

Bobbing violently in the pitch blackness and the pelting rain, the lifeboat drifted away from the *Patna*. Jim remembered that he heard the sea "hissing like twenty thousand kettles." He was so horrified that finally he jumped to save himself. He left 800 helpless Moslems to drown in the black smoke, the scalding steam, and the freezing sea. In his imagination, the *Patna*'s engines had already exploded and the shipful of praying religious pilgrims had already perished.

Jim also remembered that dawn lightened the sky above the tiny lifeboat. The rain ceased, and he saw the masthead light of the *Patna*. It did not sink. The other crewmen also saw the *Patna*'s light, as well, and they also saw Jim. During the confusion of the night, they had believed that it was their fellow crewman George, the "donkey-man," who escaped from the ship. They were enraged to see Jim; he was not one of them. He had stood apart while they struggled with the lifeboat, and during the night, he had overheard them plotting their alibis for deserting the ship. Jim would tell; he was a witness to their cowardice. They threatened to kill him, and Jim had to grab a tiller to ward off their advances. The light from the *Patna* suddenly vanished.

Survival gave Jim no happiness. His thoughts were continually darkened by a sense of the "irrational that lurks at the bottom of every thought, sentiment, sensation, emotion."

Next morning, he sat guardedly on the edge of the lifeboat, as if daring fate – or the scruffy, enraged crewmen, or the sea – to topple him over. If he could, he would swim back, witness the wreckage, and then drown himself along with the Moslems. He heard the other men absurdly feigning friendship for him and attempting all the while to rationalize their escape from the *Patna*. He was horrified when they tried to convince him that he was "one of them." He was *not* one of them. They *chose* to jump; Jim did *not* choose to jump. They chose for him. They called to him. "It was their doing as plainly as if they had reached up with a boathook and pulled [him] over."

On the verandah, Marlow is aware of the mist gathering around them, the darkness beyond, and the flickering candlelight, and he ponders how very alike truth and illusion are when compared to the mist and the candlelight and the darkness. How difficult it is to ultimately know what is "right." Even Jim said that there was not "the thickness of a sheet of paper between the right and wrong of this affair."

Jim related to Marlow his thoughts about suicide, and Marlow thinks that it is ironic that Jim should think of suicide; no one died because of Jim's actions. Suicide, Jim concluded finally, "would have ended nothing." He could also have allowed himself to be killed by the crewmen, but that would have only served their alibis of half-truths.

Jim suddenly asked Marlow for his opinion: did Marlow believe that Jim was innocent or guilty? Marlow was too stunned at the suddenness of Jim's question to answer him.

The only thing – the best thing – to do now, Jim said, was to wait –

wait for another chance to prove his worth . . . "another chance – to find out . . ."

Commentary

Chapter 10 presents the immediate horrors of Jim's jumping, and it opens with Marlow's confirming Jim's assertion at the end of Chapter 9 that Jim "had indeed jumped into an everlasting deep hole. He had tumbled from a height he could never scale again."

The first horror which Jim faces as a result of his jump is that he finds himself among the dastardly people who also deserted the ship. Jim's deepest instincts tell him that he is, if not superior, at least different from these horrible, depraved cowards, yet he too *did* desert the ship, and thus he is "one of them." They all are literally and metaphorically in the same boat, and ironically, they misidentify Jim as George, the third engineer who died (unbeknownst to them) of a heart attack.

This mistaken identity further aligns Jim with the others until they discover that it is Jim and begin to curse him. But their animosity, hatred, and threats to take his life allow Jim to again see himself as a being entirely apart (or separate) from these unethical monsters, especially as they continually call him a coward or a "murdering coward." Jim sums up the first horror of jumping as the discovery that he had joined these horrible companions. He says, "Oh yes, I know very well – I jumped. Certainly, I jumped! I told you I jumped; but I tell you they were too much for any man."

A short time after he jumped, Jim could still see the masthead light, and it terrified him to see that the ship had not sunk. Then, when he and the others saw the light disappear, they all assumed that the ship had sunk.

As we are later to hear from Captain Brierly, what happened was that the squall simply turned the ship around so that the light was no longer visible. Still, Jim had a deep desire to escape from the accursed lifeboat – to swim back and see for himself because the horror of being with the captain and the others was more horrible than possible death.

In Chapter 11, Jim again brings Marlow and us back to the matter of guilt by asking again if we wouldn't act the same as he did: "Suppose I had stuck to the ship? Well. How much longer? Say a minute – half a minute. Come. In thirty seconds, as it seemed certain then, I would have been overboard; and do you think I would not have laid hold of the first thing that came in my way – oar, life-buoy, grating – anything? Wouldn't you?" And now if Marlow even uses a euphemism, such as "And so you cleared out," Jim emphatically corrects him: "Jumped . . . Jumped, mind you."

At the end of Chapter 11, Jim is waiting "for another chance," and thus, the remainder of the novel will deal with Jim's search for another chance to prove himself to himself.

CHAPTERS 12 & 13

Summary

The narrative now focuses on what happened when Jim and the three crewmen were picked up next day by the *Avondale*. The German skipper recited the alibi agreed on by all the crewmen, except Jim. The first lifeboat, the skipper said, was lowered slowly to avoid panic, and then "the ship went down in a squall – sank like lead." Jim knew that this was a lie, but he said nothing. Still, however, he was sure that he heard hundreds of pilgrims screaming and crying out for help.

Once the men were on shore, they learned immediately that the *Patna* did not sink; it was sighted by a small French gunboat and towed to Aden. Did the *Patna's* light disappear, as the crewmen in the lifeboat seem to think it did? Yes, the wind had swung the ship's stern around, so that the lifeboat was suddenly behind the *Patna*. Thus, the *Patna* did seem to suddenly disappear.

Marlow recalls a conversation that he had, purely by chance, some time afterward; it took place in Sydney, Australia, with the French lieutenant who boarded the *Patna* the day after its officers deserted it. For thirty hours, the Frenchman remained on board while his small boat pulled the *Patna* toward Aden, two of his men ready at any minute to cut the tow lines and let the *Patna* – and all 800 Moslems – sink if the ship's stern caved in. But the *Patna's* stern did not burst, and the rescue mission was wholly uneventful, remembered by the Frenchman primarily because the religious pilgrims did not have a single drop of wine to serve him with dinner.

Marlow continued his conversation with the elderly French officer, fascinated by the man's bitterness and sadness. "I have known some brave men," the Frenchman said, but, within each one, there was always fear: "the fear – it is always there." He sighed and said that "all men are weak," but that we must each accept that truth and "live with it."

The French lieutenant left, and Marlow was alone. He shuddered as he thought of Jim working as a mere water-clerk, perhaps the most "unheroic," most unromantic work imaginable. He remembered a small, short man, "bearded to the waist like a gnome," whose soul had shrunk to the size of "a parched pea" when circumstances forced him to do menial work; yet that man proved his manhood to himself when he tried to rescue a strong-bodied, strong-willed woman who so overpowered him that they both drowned.

Marlow then returns us to the night before Jim's sentencing. That night, Marlow offered Jim a plan for escape, in addition to a letter of recommendation for a new job – plus more than 200 rupees ("A loan, of course"). Jim would have none of it. "Clear out!" he told Marlow, and Jim's face was so close that Marlow could see the soft down on Jim's smooth, young skin.

Jim said that he had to be his own witness for what he had done. "I may have jumped, but I don't run away." The knowledge that he jumped from the *Patna*, abandoning 800 people to what he was sure was certain death, was a deadly weight upon his soul. By staying to face the panel of inquiry, Jim hoped to perform an act that would partially restore his sense of self-worth.

With a miserable grin on his face and a nervous laugh, Jim dashed off then, and the night swallowed him up. Marlow was stunned. Jim had touched Marlow's "secret sensibility"; Marlow knew that he himself might have taken the money and run if he were Jim. He was awed and puzzled by such resolute idealism in one so alone and so young, "not yet four-and-twenty."

Commentary

Jim tries to explain that when the *Avondale* rescued them, he said nothing when the captain gave out the fictitious story because, after all, "I had jumped, hadn't I?" Thus after avoiding the word "jumped" for so long, now that he has actually said it, he seems to take a perverse delight in using the word. After the report of the *Patna*, Jim is exultant partly because the shouts for help that have been haunting him must have been imaginary, but nevertheless, these shouts were so piercing that he is now glad that the pilgrims were saved so that he will no longer hear their imaginary shouts. He still can't understand the sinking of the masthead (explained by Captain Brierly as a shift in the ship's position), but he knows that it too must be imaginary.

Conrad then shifts his narrative to that of the report of the French lieutenant whose gunboat rescued the *Patna*. Then Conrad shifts the novel's time sequence again – this time, to three years in the future, when Marlow encountered this same French lieutenant who had boarded the *Patna* and oversaw her towing for thirty hours without sleep or wine, but knowing that two quartermasters were standing with axes ready to cut loose the lines if the *Patna* were to begin to sink, in which case, the French lieutenant would have also have gone to his death.

And yet in Chapter 13, when Marlow and the French lieutenant discuss the events, the Frenchman does not condemn Jim for his actions. Even though he himself was there for thirty hours, he maintains that "After all, one does not die of . . . being afraid." Also, he maintains that "there is a point – there is a point – for the best of us – there is somewhere a point when you let go everything. And you have got to live with that truth – do you see?" Thus, the man who faced death for thirty hours refuses to either condemn or judge Jim.

Conrad (or Marlow) then returns to the time of the trial – just before the judging, when Marlow finally feels that Jim has suffered enough indignation and therefore offers him money (200 rupees from Captain Brierly and more from himself) so that Jim can simply leave, disappear. But Jim refuses: "I may have jumped, but I don't run away." It is as though once again his romantic nature craves added punishment and indignation.

CHAPTER 14

Summary

The day of Jim's sentencing arrived. Marlow imagined Jim on a scaffolding, ready to be beheaded. But Jim's punishment was not that romantic; still, however, it was every bit as cruel. Jim's certificate to be a British naval officer was canceled. He could never again serve aboard a ship – except as a common sailor. Jim's dream of being a ship's officer and performing all sorts of heroic deeds had been shattered. He had planned to live forever on the sea; now he had to begin a new life, with the knowledge that he had been judged unfit to be responsible for other people.

Marlow tried to talk with Jim after the sentencing, but he was too upset and dazed, and he pulled away. "Let no man . . ." he said thickly.

Marlow stared after him for only a moment; then he turned his attention to "Chester," an old, well-known roustabout sailor, who seemed anxious to talk. Chester asked Marlow if he would try to convince Jim that he had a future ahead of him if he would agree to be the chief overseer of forty coolies on a guano island that Chester planned to develop. Marlow could not imagine a worse future for Jim; he refused to even mention the job. He would not sentence Jim to such a fate.

Commentary

This chapter presents the final, "official" verdict about Jim's jumping ship, and Conrad builds up suspense for it by having the court ask a series of unimportant questions. Then we hear the final verdict: "Certificate cancelled."

Having been branded as a coward and his certificate cancelled, what worse fate could befall Jim? Conrad hints at one possible "worse" fate in the episode concerning Chester and Robinson, who are two of the most disreputable men of the South Seas—in fact, one of them, Robinson, has long been suspected of cannibalism. These two horrible creatures typify the dark powers that wait to swallow a discouraged and rejected man. They are introduced to show the change that is taking place within Marlow because Chester's suggestion fills Marlow with utter loathing.

These two unsavory men need a kind of non-person to do their dirty work—overseeing coolie labor in digging and sacking bird manure—and they feel that the horribly disgraced Jim is just such a person, or non-person. Marlow, horrified at this completely decadent, immoral proposition, will not intervene. His view of Jim does not include such depraved labors or even working with such depraved men. Marlow is clearly so deeply involved with Jim that he cannot abandon him to such degradation.

CHAPTERS 15-17

Summary

Marlow finally found Jim gazing emptily off the quay, and he told him to come to his room. Jim followed him, seemingly still in a daze. Marlow led him into his bedroom and began writing letters immediately, so that Jim could feel that he was not totally alone, but that he was sufficiently alone so that he could confront his unhappiness and despair during this darkest moment of his life.

Marlow tells us that throughout that afternoon and into the evening, he, Marlow, filled sheet after sheet of fresh paper, stopping only momentarily to notice Jim's convulsive shoulders and his struggling for breath as he stood rooted in front of a glass door. Then, suddenly, Jim opened the glass door and lurched onto the upstairs verandah, as if to throw himself off. Marlow noted his straight, resolute outline. Symbolically, it seemed as though Jim were alone, abandoned on the brink of a dark and hopeless ocean.

What would have happened if Marlow had offered Jim the job as Chester's overseer? He felt, at that moment, that he had saved Jim from what would probably have been a living death on the guano island. But, at the same time, Marlow felt that "to bury him would have been such an easy kindness." What had he saved Jim for? Marlow was aware of a sense of deep responsibility for Jim, a sense of kinship and responsibility that he could no longer ignore.

Marlow breaks the suspense and tells us that *eventually* Jim became "loved, trusted, [and] admired." He became a "legend of strength and prowess . . . the stuff of a hero." In short, Marlow says, Jim "captured much honour," meaning that Jim became a hero in the eyes of himself and others. This is what Jim desired so desperately and what he thought was denied to him because of his actions aboard the *Patna*. Jim's future, then, was not as black as he believed it was; eventually, he would perform an act of bravery that would balance and cancel out the enormous guilt that he had carried after jumping from the *Patna* and leaving 800 Moslems to what he believed was certain death.

At that moment, a violent tropical rainstorm suddenly ruptured the stillness, and Jim stepped back into the room. At last, he seemed ready to talk. Desperately, he said that a person was "bound to come upon some sort of a chance to get it all back—must!" He was determined to convince himself that he would someday have a chance to redeem himself in his own eyes, a chance to do something that would erase the blot of guilt on his character.

Marlow tried to force Jim to talk about the future – how he planned to earn money, and how he planned to pay for food and lodging. But Jim refused to talk about practical matters. "That isn't the thing," he said, and he added that it was useless for Marlow to try and convince him to accept the back pay that was still due him from the *Patna*.

Marlow found Jim's torturous soul-searching to be blindly melo-dramatic; he couldn't understand why Jim seemed determined to dwell on "some deep idea." He sensed intuitively that he himself could prob-ably never heal the agony in Jim's "wounded spirit."

Nevertheless, Marlow told Jim that he had written a letter of recommendation to a man who would give Jim a second chance. He stressed that he, Marlow, had faith in Jim's goodness and promise – even if Jim did not; he was making himself "unreservedly responsible" for Jim.

After awhile, the rain stopped and Jim leapt up. "It is noble of you!" he shouted. Marlow was so stunned that he wondered if Jim were mocking him. Jim seemed madly exhilarated. But the young man was not mocking Marlow's offer. His eyes were bright, and his voice was a stammer of half-sentences. He was agitated and seemingly wild with newfound confidence. "You have given me a clean slate," he announced to Marlow.

Commentary

After showing Jim at his lowest point in the preceding chapter, Marlow tells us that he lived to see Jim "loved, trusted, admired, with a legend of strength and prowess forming round his name as though he had been the stuff of a hero." It is as though Marlow is telling us to *wait* – because his evaluation of Jim is correct. That is, Jim is indeed one of us. He also lets us know that had he not interceded between Chester and Jim, then he would never have seen Jim again because he learns later that the men on Chester's guano enterprise disappeared.

And yet, Chester, and all that pertains to him, is important because it shows Marlow's development. Marlow still feels that Jim is con-cerned not so much with his guilt as he is with the humiliating and treacherous "jump" and its shameful consequences. Jim is seen here writhing in the agonies of romantic melancholy with his "refined sensibilities and his fine feelings, fine longings – a sort of sublimated, idealized selfishness"; that is, Jim is too "fine a fellow" to throw over to Chester and his kind.

These descriptions of Jim prepare us for Stein's firm statement that Jim is a romantic. And certainly in the romantic tradition, Jim's raging emotions within are symbolically reflected in the raging storm outside. Throughout these scenes, Marlow watches Jim writhe and squirm in agony like one of Stein's impaled beetles, but then Marlow is also impaled on the sharp point of his own new affection for Jim and the sense of his responsibility for Jim.

Since the trial is now over, Marlow turns to practical matters (Jim won't consider the horror of accepting his back pay from the *Patna*), and when Marlow volunteers to help, Jim responds by saying, "You can't." Of course, Marlow meant "help with practical matters," but Jim means help in an entirely different sense – in assuaging his feelings of disgrace and guilt. Thus, when Marlow tells Jim that he is writing to a man in Jim's behalf, Jim's appreciation is immense – mainly because he now realizes that there is someone who still cares for him, or believes in him, a fact which gives Jim a new confidence in himself. Jim's soaring gratitude and unbounded delight as Marlow unfolds his plan indicate a relief and a deliverance from an alternative so forbidding as to suggest nothing short of death itself.

CHAPTERS 18 & 19

Summary

Six months later, while Marlow was in Hong Kong, he received a letter from a Mr. Denver, the owner of a rice mill, the friend to whom he recommended Jim. Denver, an eccentric, middle-aged bachelor, wrote quietly but glowingly about Jim; he was especially fond of Jim's quality of "freshness" – his quiet, naive, generous nature.

Marlow smiled to himself. He was right to send Jim to his friend. Perhaps, he speculated, Jim might inherit a good sum of money from the old bachelor.

Marlow then made a trip northward, and when he returned to Hong Kong, another letter from Denver was awaiting him. Denver was furious: Jim had vanished.

Also in the pile of letters, there was a note from Jim. He was work-ing in a seaport town seven hundred miles south, and he wrote that he had no choice; he had to leave Denver's rice mill. The second engineer from the *Patna* unexpectedly turned up at Denver's mill and was given temporary employment. Shortly thereafter, this man began making insinuations about Jim's past, threatening blackmail unless he were put on full-time at the mill. Jim said that he could "no longer stand the familiarity of the little beast," so he left. He asked Marlow for another letter of recommendation. He had found temporary work as a "runner," or a water-clerk, for a ship-chandler, and he wanted permanence as soon as possible.

Some months later, Marlow was in port and met Jim. He seemed to be happy and busy and popular. Marlow had a good feeling about the future of the young man. Then, six months afterward, Marlow was again in port and inquired about Jim at Egstrom & Blake, the ship-chandlers who employed him. Egstrom told Marlow that sud-denly one day, Jim left—without an explanation. Jim was his best runner, he says; there was no better water-clerk in port than Jim. He told Marlow that he offered Jim more money, emphasizing that business was exceptionally good: "This business ain't going to sink," Egstrom told Jim.

Marlow asked pointedly if anyone mentioned anything about the *Patna* just prior to Jim's disappearance. Egstrom remembered that one of the old sea captains had expounded on the whole disgraceful business of the *Patna*. Marlow told the ship-chandler that that ex-plained it: Jim was the first mate of the *Patna* on the night of "the incident." The ship-chandler was puzzled. "Who the devil cares about that?" he asked. Then he added that if Jim were that sensitive about his past, then even the earth itself "wouldn't be big enough" for him to hide in.

Jim continued running, and it was not long before he became known as "a rolling stone," Marlow says. In fact, Jim even became "notorious" within the sphere of about three thousand miles that he traversed. All around that area, people recognized his name and knew all about the secret that he considered so shameful. Jim, of course, never dreamed that so many people knew so many details about the secret that he kept so tightly hidden within his breast.

One night, however, during a brawl in a hotel billiards room, Jim got an inkling that a lot of people knew a great deal more about him than he cared for them to know. He was playing billiards with a Navy officer, a cross-eyed Dane who was employed by the Royal Siamese Navy. The fellow had drunk too much, and he made a slurring reference to Jim's part in the *Patna* fiasco.

Jim reacted like a madman. He broke a billiard cue in half and then threw the naval officer off the verandah and into the Menam River.

Marlow realized that after that incident, Jim was no doubt beginning to think that all jobs would eventually be dead ends for him. There would be money paid to him for a job well done, but the situation itself would never be satisfying. What Jim needed was a challenge for his soul, not a job for his hands.

Marlow, therefore, went to see "the most trustworthy man" he knew—a Mr. Stein. Stein was very wealthy and very respected, and he had trading posts all over the world. Moreover, he was a learned man—in particular, an internationally known expert on beetles and butterflies. Marlow felt that it was time to discuss Jim's problems with another person, someone who could see the enormous guilt that Jim insisted on living with. Marlow was looking for someone who could offer Jim a job that would be entirely different from the sort of menial laboring that might lend itself to ridicule and third-class status.

Commentary

In these two chapters, Marlow relates three episodes involving Jim, and the episodes occurred at immense geographical distances from each other. In each case where some connection or comment was made about the *Patna* episode, Jim would literally flee. For example, in his first job where he had earned the respect of his employer, Mr. Denver stood to reap great financial rewards; the happenstance appearance of the second mate was bad enough, but when this second mate tried to become intimate with Jim, Jim could not "stand the familiarity of the little beast."

After all, Jim was a gentleman, and furthermore, after the sinking of the *Patna*, the second mate and his fellow officers had considered killing Jim. Likewise, at Jim's next job—one in which he was extremely successful and well liked—he fled immediately when someone began discussing the *Patna* episode, and his final adventure was with the Dane in the Siamese Navy. All three of these episodes represent what must have been dozens more (as Marlow says, "More than

I could count on the fingers of my two hands"), and thus Jim's almost obsessive, almost pathological sense of guilt has made him known over thousands of miles all through the South Pacific.

It is ironic that Jim feels his guilt more than other people. His innate sensitivity makes him feel that everyone condemns him, and then we hear that Egstrom did not care at all. Egstrom says, "And who the devil cares about that?" Furthermore, the physical attack on the Dane represents the one time that Jim did *not* behave as though he was "one of us."

After one episode when Marlow brings Jim aboard his ship, Jim constantly remains below deck and is quiet and reticent. Note that when Marlow asks him if he would like to go to California, Jim responds, "What difference would it make?" In other words, Jim cannot escape from himself even if it be across continents and oceans — instead, he is looking for an opportunity to prove himself to himself.

CHAPTERS 20 & 21

Summary

Marlow entered Stein's house late in the evening and was struck immediately by the dramatic figure of the old man, sitting at his desk, washed in the glow of a single spot of light in the darkened room. Then Marlow's eyes caught the outlines of the cases containing Stein's hobbies. He was surrounded by catacombs of beetles and long glass cases of butterflies. "Marvelous," Stein whispered over one of the cases of butterflies.

Marlow admired one butterfly in particular, and Stein told him that a butterfly was a masterpiece of nature. In comparison, man was amazing, but he was no masterpiece. Then Stein told Marlow how he had acquired this particular specimen.

One day while on the outpost where he lived for so many years, he was called away to a meeting. The summons was fraudulent, however, and Stein encountered an ambush. But he feigned death and was able to kill three soldiers and drive off the others. He looked at one of the men whom he had killed, and suddenly, a shadow seemed to pass over the dead man's forehead. It was this very butterfly, a particularly rare variety that he had dreamed of and searched for all his life. Suddenly, here it was, fluttering slowly away from the corpse of a man who had tried to murder him. Acting just as instantly as he had during the ambush attempt, he clapped his hat over the butterfly.

Immediately, Stein was so stunned by his good fortune that his knees collapsed under him. Life had reached its climax for him at that moment. Stein wanted nothing more. He had been victorious against his enemies, he had a beloved wife and daughter, and now he had the butterfly of his dreams.

Marlow told Stein that he had come to him to discuss another kind of rare specimen—a rare specimen of a man. Then he began describing Jim's unusual nature. Stein murmured that he understood Jim well: Jim was a romantic. Marlow accepted the diagnosis immediately. But what was to be done to cure him? he asked Stein. Stein answered that it was futile to try and "cure" a romantic. Instead, one should focus on helping him to understand how to live with his romanticism—that is, "how to live. . . . How to be. Ach! How to be."

A man, he said, is born and it is as though he has fallen into a sea, a dream. And if he tries to crawl out of his dream, he drowns. To triumph in this sea of dreams, he must *immerse* himself in the destructive element and battle it into submission in his own individual way. "Reality" is only a dream; we should treat it with great seriousness, and yet we should hold ourselves at a distance from it, knowing that none of it matters ultimately. Thus, we are prevented from "taking matters too much to heart."

Jim's problem, Stein said, was taking matters "too much to heart." He proposed that, for the present, he and Marlow should retire. In the morning, they would speak of "practical" solutions to Jim's problem. They would not try to cure Jim of his romanticism; instead, they would search for ways that they could give Jim a chance to live successfully with his romanticism.

Marlow begins Chapter 21 by explaining where the settlement of Patusan is. It is a little-known post in the Malay Islands, forty miles inland and upriver, controlled by three warring factions. It is known to very few people in the mercantile world.

Two years after Jim accepted Stein's offer of resident manager of the trading post, Marlow went to visit him in Patusan, and he marvelled at the change that had been wrought in the young man. Clearly, Jim had accomplished much and had regulated much in Patusan. Marlow, of course, was filled with happiness. Jim's victory over his self-punishing romanticism had been an excellent triumph.

And it was a victory, Marlow says, "in which I had taken my part." Jim had achieved greatness. In fact, he had achieved such greatness that most of those who heard about it could never fathom it because their imaginations were too starved and too dull.

Comparing Jim, who was once so flawed as to seem suicidal, with the masses of other men, Marlow says that Jim was like a "light of glamour created in the shock of trifles, as amazing as the glow of sparks struck from a cold stone – and as short-lived, alas!"

Commentary

In Chapter 19, Marlow had decided to take Jim's problems to a wealthy merchant named Stein, a respected and trustworthy man. Stein was also a world-renowned collector of rare butterflies and beetles. Marlow (Conrad) now offers us a history (or background) to Mr. Stein.

The main point of this digression is to show us Stein's reaction to treachery, ambush, and betrayal as opposed to the capture of the most beautiful butterfly in the world. In other words, Stein thinks nothing of being betrayed, ambushed, and shot at by would-be assassins (or even deceptively killing some of his would-be assassins), but when, in the next moment, he finds one of the rarest butterflies in the world, his knees collapse with wonderment and joy. Therefore, this digression shows Stein to be probably one of the most magnificent romantics in the world, and thus, he will recognize immediately that Jim is also a romantic. Indeed, after hearing Jim's story, Stein immediately pronounces: "He is romantic – romantic."

Clearly, Stein identifies with Jim and thinks of how many wonderful opportunities have come his way that he has missed while Jim has missed *only one* – the chance to be the hero of the *Patna* episode instead of its scapegoat. Stein then suggests to Marlow that their problem is *not* how to cure Jim, but instead, how to teach him to live (practically and otherwise) with himself.

Chapter 21 introduces us to Patusan, where it is decided that Jim will be sent to replace the present, dishonest manager. The importance of Patusan is that it is the most isolated place in that part of the world. Consequently, it will allow Jim to be extremely isolated and so preoccupied that he will not have time to confront himself with massive attacks of guilt and self-recrimination.

At the end of this chapter, we gain somewhat of an understanding of why Marlow has taken such pains with Jim: Marlow believes that "We exist only in so far as we hang together," and since Jim is one of us, it becomes necessary for Marlow and Stein (and, previously, the others – Mr. Denver, Egstrom, and De Jongh) to look after Jim.

CHAPTERS 22 & 23

Summary

Patusan, we are told, was often used by adventurers to satisfy either their greed or their need to perform heroic deeds. It was savage country, shut off from the rest of the world. A man could feel as though he were a "hero" if he went there to go "into the bush" – that is, to ravage Patusan's treasure, which was pepper. Men had often died in Patusan attempting a perilous quest for pepper, for at one time, pepper was almost as valuable as pearls. One day, however, pepper lost its aura of rarity, and as the narrator says, "Nobody cares for it now." Today, wealth is no longer flowing out of Patusan, and the bones of its anonymous "heroes" are lying in scattered heaps, bleaching on sunlit beaches. Marlow marvels at the bizarre, absurd lengths to which some men will go to achieve money and transient glory.

When Jim went to Patusan, Marlow says, the only people fighting over Patusan were the diverse uncles of the Sultan, himself "an imbecile youth with two thumbs on his left hand." The worst of the uncles was Rajah Allang, a "dirty little used-up old man with evil eyes and a weak mouth."

Marlow remembers Jim's reaction when he first told him about Patusan. Initially, Jim had felt a kind of "weary resignation," but that attitude was gradually replaced by "surprise, interest, wonder, and by boyish eagerness." This was the chance Jim had been dreaming of!

Marlow emphasized to Jim that this venture would be "his [Jim's] own doing." Jim would be wholly responsible. The young man was filled with impulsive and inarticulate joy. He didn't mind going into a wilderness. He was eager to do so! The outside world would never know that he had ever existed. At last, he would finally have "nothing but the soles of his two feet to stand on." Marlow cautioned Jim to use prudence in this new venture, but Jim was filled with so much exuberance that he flung himself out of the room before Marlow could finish speaking.

Jim stated that he never wanted to go back to England, a desire that Marlow found unimaginable. Never? he asked him. Never, Jim emphasized. He was adamant about his decision: " 'Never,' he repeated dreamily . . . and then flew into sudden activity."

With Marlow's help, Jim finally got packed. Then, at the last moment before Jim's rowers had cast off, Marlow clamored onto Jim's ship and talked briefly to Jim's half-caste captain, who seemed to be a lunatic. The man said that he intended to take Jim to the mouth of the river leading into Patusan, but that he had no intention of going any farther upriver. Patusan was too dangerous; it was like a "cage of beasts made ravenous by long impenitence," he said, and in a mock pantomime, he dramatically stabbed himself in the back.

Behind the captain, Marlow saw Jim suddenly appear, smiling silently and raising a hand to check Marlow's horror of the adventure that was about to begin. Then a heavy boom swung around, and Jim and Marlow clasped each other's hands. Marlow awkwardly called Jim "dear boy," and Jim half-uttered "old man."

Yet, Marlow says, there was in their embarrassed goodbyes, "a moment of real and profound intimacy, unexpected and short-lived like a glimpse of some everlasting, saving truth." The ship cast off, and Jim raised his cap above his head and waved it broadly to Marlow, calling out indistinctly, "You – shall – hear – of – me."

Commentary

Again, Conrad (and Marlow) lets us know that at an earlier time, Patusan was famous for its vast treasure of pepper, but now that pepper is not so important, Patusan has lost much of its influence as an important trading center. In fact, the reader often wonders (and is never told precisely) what it is that justifies Stein's still retaining a trading post there.

In this chapter, we also hear of the immense danger for strangers to travel to Patusan; the "wary captain" who is to take Jim to Patusan refuses to go any farther than the mouth of the river; he explains to Marlow that he already sees Jim as a dead man. Part of the danger is a man named Rajah Allang (an evil man who will capture Jim upon his arrival and who will be a force for Jim to contend with for a long time).

Jim, however, welcomes to the point of ecstasy the opportunity to simply fade from civilization, to enter Patusan and let the veil of civilization forever close behind him. He welcomes the opportunity

48

to "jump into the unknown" and "achieve his disappearance" from all of the known world.

Thus, Conrad continues his metaphor of "jumping"—that is, just as Jim's jump from the *Patna* was a jump into an unknown part of himself, his "jump" here, into an unknown part of the world (into Patusan), is an equivalent jump into the unknown. "Once he got in, it would be for the outside world as though he had never existed. He would have nothing but the soles of his two feet to stand upon."

We further see Stein as the complete romantic, and his romantic nature is further revealed in the generous provisions that he is ready to make for this youth, whose story has captured his own romantic imagination to the point that he is ready to bestow much of his fortune on Jim.

In Chapter 23, we are told about the ring which old Doramin gave to Stein as a parting symbol of their eternal friendship. Jim is to take Stein's ring to Doramin, and it will insure him protection by the great chief ("The ring was a sort of credential"). This, of course, is the ring which will figure so prominently in Jim's tragic death at the end of the narrative.

Although Jim is wildly enthusiastic about his future fortunes—to Marlow, Jim seems filled with romantic posturing to the point of being melodramatic. But even now, Marlow doesn't fully understand the nature of the weight that Jim feels, a weight so heavy that Marlow doesn't understand Jim when Jim mentions that once he is in Patusan, he will never want to come out again. When Marlow asserts that "if you only live long enough, you will want to come back," Jim virtually ignores him and dismisses Marlow's comment with the remark, "Come back to what?" For Jim, the civilized world has no hold on him. He is no longer a part of the civilized world. For Jim, this is his "magnificent chance" to prove his own worth to himself.

CHAPTERS 24 & 25

Summary

Two years later, Marlow visited Patusan, carrying a message from Stein to Jim, which instructed Jim to set up a proper trading post. Marlow marveled at the misty ocean, the swampy plains, and the far-off blue mountain peaks. He stopped at a fishing village and engaged an old man who seemed to be the village's head man to pilot him upriver.

Most of the old man's talk on the way up was about "Tuan Jim," or Lord Jim, a man of whom he spoke with warm, glowing familiarity and simple awe. Clearly, all the villagers loved and trusted Jim. In fact, most of them believed that he had supernatural powers. In the short time that Jim had lived in Patusan, many legends had grown up around him. Marlow was told, for example, that on the day Jim arrived, the tide rose two hours before its usual time in order to carry Jim upriver.

Later, when Jim and Marlow were sitting on the verandah of Jim's house, Marlow listened to Jim's version of his arrival at Patusan. Jim had sat on the tin luggage box during the entire voyage, his unloaded revolver on his lap. It was an exhausting journey, he said, the boat scissoring through crocodiles, and the jungle seeming to be continually formidable and ominous. Near the end of the journey, he dozed. When he awakened, he noticed that his three paddlers had disappeared. Almost immediately, he was taken prisoner by armed men who escorted him to Rajah Allang, the little "used-up" despot.

Jim paused, and Marlow reflected that the "experiment" had turned out remarkably well. There was none of Jim's former hypersensitivity to guilt and anguish. Instead, Jim seemed to have conquered his urge to punish himself. He had won the trust, the friendship, and the love of the natives. And he had even attained a kind of fame.

As Jim talked to Marlow, Marlow noted Jim's deep and fierce love for the land. To leave Patusan would be, Jim said, "harder than dying." According to Marlow, Jim had become both Patusan's master and its captive.

On their way to meet Rajah Allang, Jim pointed out to Marlow a filthy stockade in which he was held captive for three days. On the third day, he said, he did the only thing he could do: he tried to escape.

At that moment of their conversation, however, they met Rajah Allang. Marlow says that he was immediately impressed with the man's respectful attitude toward Jim, who only two years before had been this man's prisoner. Jim and Marlow witnessed Rajah Allang's solving a village problem, and then they were offered coffee. Marlow was reluctant to drink his, fearing that it might be poisoned, but Jim unperturbedly sipped his coffee.

Later, Jim told Marlow that he had to constantly prove that he was worthy of their trust. He had to drink their coffee. He had to take the risk – "take it every month" – the natives trusted him to do that. Jim said that Rajah Allang was most likely afraid of Jim precisely because Jim was *not* afraid to drink the Rajah's coffee.

After Jim escaped from Rajah Allang's stockade two years ago and found safety with Doramin, he learned about the warring factions that seemed to rule Patusan. They were:

(1) Rajah Allang, from whom Jim had just escaped; he brought blood and fiery destruction on any villager who attempted to trade with the outside world. Rajah Allang wanted to be the exclusive trader in Patusan.

(2) Stein's friend Doramin was the "second chief" in Patusan. Years ago, he was elected by "his people," immigrants from the Dutch West Indies; his party opposed Rajah Allang's terrorizing monopoly on trading.

(3) The other "leader" of Patusan was a half-breed Arab, Sherif Ali. He incited the interior tribes with religious fervor, and his followers practiced guerrilla warfare. He had a camp on the summit of one of Patusan's twin mountains, where he hung over the village "like a hawk over a poultry yard." Of the three powers that controlled Patusan, Sherif Ali was the most dangerous – to Rajah Allang's people, and to the Bugis Malays under old Doramin.

Commentary

Again in these chapters, Conrad (or Marlow) skips about from past time to present time (two years later). We witness a scene when Marlow visits Jim, and then the narrator returns to a past time, when Jim first arrived in Patusan.

Marlow even hints of future occurrences and tells the story of Jim's arrival from a distance of many years, and so it seems natural to him (and, of course, to Conrad) to call up, first, one experience and then another – without due regard for their time sequences.

By the time of Marlow's arrival, the natives are calling Jim "Tuan Jim" or, in English, Lord Jim, and we are told that Jim has won their respect and, in some cases, their awe; already, many legendary stories have grown up around Lord Jim. Without our knowing how Lord Jim accomplished it, we are informed that he had indeed achieved a type of greatness – complete trust and ultimate respect in this outpost. "He was approaching greatness as genuine as any man ever achieved."

When Jim first arrived, we hear from Marlow (who is narrating what Jim told him) that Jim had been held captive for three days, and Marlow points out that had he (Jim) been killed then, the entire province of Patusan "would have been the loser." Even Jim recognizes his greatness and appreciates the fact that now, "there is not one [house] where I am not trusted." Lord Jim has at last, finally, found his niche in the universe, and he will never leave Patusan, the place where he is honored and trusted, respected and loved.

In addition to Jim's newfound self-assurance and happiness, Marlow noticed other differences in Jim. He was now more intellectually alert; there was an eloquence and "a dignity in his constitutional reticence" and a "high seriousness" in his actions that showed "how deeply, how solemnly" he felt about his work at Patusan. Marlow concluded that Jim had indeed found himself.

When Jim took Marlow to the place where Rajah Allang, who had held him prisoner, lived, Jim showed great courage in drinking coffee once a month with the Rajah – even though he knew that it might be poisoned.

Lord Jim then told Marlow of his escape – of another "jump," which this time led him to a bog where, for awhile, he was stuck in mud and slime. When he emerged, he was symbolically covered with filth, but even in this disgusting condition, he ran to Doramin's stockade, where he showed him the ring and was accepted into Doramin's family, thus symbolically emerging from the filth and slime to begin anew a new, clean, productive life. The symbolism is obvious: the "jump" that takes Jim deep into the vile slime and mud of the creek represents the jump from the *Patna* which immersed Jim deep into vile shame and everlasting remorse.

CHAPTERS 26 & 27

Summary

At this point, Marlow interrupts his narrative in order to introduce us to the incredible person of Doramin, the longtime friend of Stein. Doramin, Marlow says, was remarkable. He was an imposing, monumental hulk of a man, with proud, staring eyes. In contrast, his wife was light, delicate, quick, and a little witchlike, despite the fact that she was always fussing over him.

Their only son, Dain Waris, was Jim's best friend. He was married at eighteen and was now twenty-five. He was attentive and deeply respectful of his parents, and he loved Jim and trusted him implicitly and without reservation. Because of their deep, warm, war-comrade sort of friendship, each of the men, Marlow says, was a "captive" of the other, just as Marlow observed earlier that Jim was a "captive" of Patusan.

These, then, were Jim's most trusted allies, those to whom he would owe complete allegiance when he initiated his plan to bring peace to Patusan. He had no other choice than to try and bring peace to the island, he told Marlow; in fact, he felt compelled to try and bring peace to the island.

"It seemed to come to me. All at once I saw what I had to do." Everywhere that Jim looked, he saw fear. He realized that he would have to do something dramatic and daring in order to control both Rajah Allang and Sherif Ali. In a moment of almost mystical vision, Jim realized that he had "the power to make peace"; that was to be his purpose in Patusan.

His plan was bold and audacious, but he believed that he could persuade enough of the natives who supported Doramin to help him destroy Sherif Ali's stockade. Not surprisingly, Dain Waris was the first native to support Jim's plan.

First, two old and rusty "seven-pound brass cannons" had to be hauled by ingenious means up one of the mountains. From that vantage point, Jim could blow up Sherif Ali's camp on the other mountain, and then a large group of men would storm through the remains of Sherif Ali's camp.

The men worked all night long in a superhuman effort to pull the enormously heavy cannons up the mountain, the noses of them "tearing slowly through the bushes, like a wild pig rooting its way in the undergrowth." Sherif Ali watched Jim and the natives and thought that they were idiotic. But old Doramin was so fascinated by Jim's plan that he had himself carried up the hill in his armchair so that he could watch. Jim figured that if his plan didn't work, Doramin had decided that he wanted to die on the mountain. Nobody, Jim says, truly believed that his plan would work – except Jim himself.

Marlow says that after Jim's dramatically successful rout of Sherif Ali, he became a legend in Patusan; the natives believed that he had supernatural powers. Stories were told about Jim's literally carrying the enormous brass cannons up the mountain on his back. Jim laughed a "Homeric peal of laughter" when he related this tale to Marlow. Speaking of the enormous explosion, he said, "You should have seen the splinters fly."

Jim and Dain Waris were the first ones to invade the stockade, which was built so flimsily that it almost fell down before them. Instantly, Dain Waris saved Jim's life from the spear of a "pockmarked tattooed native."

The third man into the ruins of the stockade was young Tamb' Itam, and from that moment on, Tamb' Itam became inseparable from Jim. Symbolically, he would follow Jim everywhere, like, Marlow says, "a morose shadow of darkness." Very soon, Jim made him "head-man," and all Patusan respected him and accepted him as a man of much influence.

The rout was complete, but afterwards, it was, Jim said, "an awful responsibility," for when success came, Jim realized almost instantly that his soul had been absorbed "into the innermost life of the people." He was the epitomy of a hero to the Patusan people. He had their "blind trust." They were totally dependent on him. Their dependence was Jim's total responsibility. Jim was suddenly granted power. Thus, it was no wonder that Jim told Marlow that he had a sudden, jarring sense of isolation and loneliness. He had become "an exceptional man." Every word that he spoke was "the one truth of every passing day." From now on, the natives would look to Jim for Truth.

Commentary

Chapter 26 establishes the fact that Doramin, his wife, and their son Dain Waris are a very closely knit family, with Dain Waris being the son of their later life. Likewise, Conrad (Marlow) is anxious to establish the close bond of friendship that exists between Lord Jim and Dain Waris. It should also perhaps be noted that although we are constantly told about the depth of this friendship between Dain Waris and Lord Jim, we seldom see it in operation except for the fact that Dain Waris was the first person to endorse Lord Jim's plan to bombard Sherif Ali's stronghold, and that it was Dain Waris who saved Jim's life. Of course, we are also told that Dain Waris "not only trusted Jim, he understood him."

The emphasis upon the closeness between Doramin and his son and upon the close friendship between Lord Jim and Dain Waris fore-shadows the final moments in Lord Jim's life. Likewise, the pair of magnificent pistols on Doramin's knees will play a sinister part later on. These are the "immense flintlock pistols" which Stein gave Doramin in exchange for the ring which Doramin gave Stein, and these are the pistols which will be the instruments of death for Jim.

Jim's desire to bring peace to the land becomes tantamount in his mind. His own fate and, later, his fame are both based upon the success of his attack against Sherif Ali. After the success of the bold plan to take the cannons up the mountain and after his routing Sherif Ali, Jim's fame becomes so great that some of the natives even report that he carried the cannons singlehandedly on his own back. After this military success, Jim's fame places him in a position where he is expected to settle everything—even divorce cases: "His word decided everything." Jim's victory, we realize, gave him a firm sense of his own worth and value: "Thus he illustrated the moral effect of his victory in war. It was in truth immense."

CHAPTERS 28–30

Summary

After Sherif Ali was routed, there was no further trouble from Rajah Allang. He immediately flung himself face down on his bamboo floor and moaned in fear for hours on end. Meanwhile, Jim conferred with Dain Waris, and they appointed new head-men for the villages; Jim had taken control of the area.

Old Doramin took great pride in the peace that Jim brought to Patusan, and he dreamed of someday seeing his son, Dain Waris, as the ultimate ruler of Patusan. This was his secret ambition, his single most secret obsession, in fact, and he had unbounded confidence in Jim's role, regarding Dain Waris' fate.

Marlow tried to assure Doramin and his wife that Jim would stay on in Patusan, but they could not believe that he would do so. They wanted to know why Jim would want to stay; no other white man had ever done so. Surely, said Doramin's wife, Jim had a home and kinsmen—a mother, perhaps? Marlow was unsuccessful in trying to convince them of Jim's decision to stay at Patusan forever.

Marlow then turns to the story of Jim's beloved Jewel, a young woman who is three-quarters white. Jewel had lived all her life at Patusan. Her stepfather was a white man, a Portuguese named Cornelius, and he was Jim's predecessor in the trading post. He was the most slinking, slimy, amoral man in the entire settlement. He was without any honor or character.

Jim placed great value on Jewel; he married her in a native ceremony, and we hear how they walked "side by side, openly, he holding her arm under his – pressed to his side – thus – in a most extraordinary way."

Cornelius was not happy that Jim had come to Patusan. He began to creep around, continually "slinking in the neighbourhood with that peculiar twist of his mouth as if he were perpetually on the point of gnashing his teeth." To Cornelius, Jim had not come to merely take Patusan from him, but already he had begun to also take Jewel from him.

Marlow says that what he remembers most clearly about Jewel was the "even, olive pallor" of her skin and the "intense blue-black gleams of her hair." Also, she wore a small crimson cap far back on her head. She was a curious mixture of charm and shyness and audacity, and she was obviously devoted to Jim; "her tenderness hovered over him like a flutter of wings." It seemed, Marlow says, as if she were always "ready to make a footstool of her head for his [Jim's] feet."

Cornelius' house was in a shambles when Jim came to live there. Half the roof had fallen in, and all of Stein's account books were torn, and there was nothing in the storehouse but rats. It was unpleasant, Jim said, and what made it worse was the fact that, during his first six weeks there, he kept hearing rumors that Rajah Allang planned to kill him, which of course, was very possible, for, as Jim said, "I couldn't see what there was to prevent him if he really had made up his mind to have me killed."

Jim tried to explain to Marlow why he had decided to remain at Patusan. Of course, he said, there was Jewel, and she was treated horribly by her stepfather. Cornelius would scream at her, curse her dead mother, and finally he would chase Jewel around the house, flinging mud at her. Such cruelty, Jim said, was "a strange thing to come upon in a wilderness." Jim was finally so exasperated by Jewel's stepfather's behavior that he told her that he was willing to kill Cornelius. Then Jewel told him a curious thing: she herself could easily kill Cornelius "with her own hands," but she knew how "intensely wretched" Cornelius was with himself.

Lying on his back one night, on a thin mat, Jim saw an omen:

"a star suddenly twinkled through a hole in the roof." Instantly, Jim knew the real reason for his staying on at Patusan. He would rid Patusan of the evil Sherif Ali. Jim knew that he had to make solid plans for overcoming Sherif Ali in his hilltop stockade "roost" above Patusan. He would destroy this Arab "who lurked above the town like a hawk above a chicken yard." Jim envisioned cannons mounted on the top of the hill opposite Sherif Ali's stockade. He became so excited and possessed by the idea that he told Jewel about it. She listened reverently to Jim, clapping her hands softly and whispering her admiration for his vision.

Commentary

Even though Jim becomes the most respected person in Patusan, being called "Tuan Jim," or Lord Jim, Doramin shows no sense of jealousy even though Doramin's most secret desire is to have his son Dain Waris become the chief ruler of Patusan. Part of Doramin's lack of jealousy, of course, stems from the fact that both he and his wife know that no white man has ever stayed in Patusan for longer than a few years, unless they were evil, vicious, spiteful, and cruel — such as the wicked and unprincipled Cornelius.

Jim, however, basking in the glory of his recent triumphs, cannot tell the people of Patusan that he is, in the eyes of the outside world, a disgrace who can never be accepted, and thus, he can never return to that society. In addition to Doramin's wife, then, who cannot believe that Jim has no mother, no one at all to return to, later Jewel, Jim's wife, will also have difficulty believing that Jim will not leave her someday.

This brings Marlow to the subject of the romantic love that developed between Jim and Cornelius' stepdaughter. Their love, from the start, was imbued with "a romantic conscience," and Jim even translated her Malay name into the English name "Jewel," meaning any gem of precious quality. Not only was their marriage performed in the native style, but their union was highly successful. It was also highly unique because Jim and Jewel would walk publicly hand-in-hand or arm-in-arm; normally, a Malay woman was supposed to walk behind her lord and master and was considered to be inferior to her husband. Furthermore, we later learn that when Jim had to be away from the village, Jewel was placed in charge of valuable property, such as the ammunition room.

Chapter 29 presents more of Jewel's background and reinforces what we have already been told about her total and complete devotion to Lord Jim—a devotion that is equaled only by Tamb' Itam's loyalty to Jim. The depth of the devotion of these two people to Jim will later account for their inability to understand Jim's decision not to flee after the terrible tragedy at the end of the novel.

In contrast to the purity and beauty of Jewel's and Tamb' Itam's characters is the vileness of Cornelius, Jewel's stepfather. "His slow, laborious walk resembled the creeping of a repulsive beetle, the legs alone moving with horrid industry while the body glided evenly. . . . [He was so] loathsome, abject and disgusting" that Marlow could not stand to even be around him. Conrad's graphic description of Cornelius prepares the reader for his vicious and cowardly behavior at the end of the novel.

Chapter 30 continues to present Cornelius' atrocious behavior, especially his disgraceful treatment of Jewel. Yet, ironically, it is in the midst of the horror of Cornelius' presence that Jim suddenly conceives of a plan to free Patusan of the wicked Sherif Ali—a plan which we have already seen was successful.

CHAPTERS 31–33

Summary

The next day, Jim spent a long time with Doramin, the old *nakhoda*, trying to impress on him and the principal men of the Bugis community the absolute necessity for immediate and vigorous action in order to counter Sherif Ali.

Meanwhile, Sherif Ali's men strutted about, "haughtily in white cloaks," spreading the rumor that Rajah Allang intended to join them in raiding and defeating the Bugis once and for all. The attack seemed imminent, and terror among the natives was intense and widespread.

Jim returned home at sunset, pleased at having convinced Doramin of his plan to rout Sherif Ali. Now he had "irretrievably committed" the Bugis to action. Now, also, Jim had committed himself; in fact, all of the responsibility for success was "on his own head." And yet he was elated and lighthearted with the fantastic possibility of his vision.

In the middle of a deep sleep that night, Jim was awakened by Jewel. She put his revolver into his hand and insisted that he get up.

Four men, she said, were waiting to kill him. Then she took him to one of the storehouses.

Jim sighed. He was tired of these alarms, and he was angry with Jewel for her increasing anxiety. But he pushed open the door of the dungeon-like ruin of a storehouse anyway. At first, he saw nothing – an empty wooden crate, and a litter of rags and straw. For days, he had been living with a heavy weight on his soul; if only there had been something here – a trace or a sign of someone. But there was nothing.

Suddenly, Jewel shouted at Jim to defend himself, and in the pale light, he saw the gleam of a pair of eyes within a heap of mats. Jim yelled for the man to come out, and a half-naked, glistening native pounced toward Jim, the blade of his knife above his head. Jim felt utter relief. He let the man come toward him until he could see his dilated nostrils and his wide eyes. Then he fired, his bullet exploding inside the man's mouth and disappearing through the back of his head.

Afterward, Jim was strangely calm. He felt "appeased, without rancour, without uneasiness." He stepped over the body and routed out three other naked figures, crawling forward from under the mats and holding out their empty hands.

Jim led the prisoners out into the night, and Jewel followed, her white nightgown trailing and her black hair falling to her waist. At the edge of the river bank, Jim stopped. He told the men to take his greetings to Sherif Ali, and then he ordered them all to "Jump!"

Afterward, when he and Jewel were alone on the river bank, Jim told Marlow that never before had he realized how dearly he loved Jewel. "More than I can tell," Jim said; to him, his love for Jewel was "idyllic, a little solemn, and also true." In addition, Jim expressed his almost disbelief in the natives' complete trust of him. He knew that he was equated with what was "true" and "brave" and "just," and yet he knew his own secret nature – that is, he knew how utterly he had failed, once.

Later, after sundown, Marlow was stopped by Jewel. She wanted "assurance" from Marlow, "a statement, a promise, an explanation." Her life had been a puzzle and a living hell – until Jim's appearance. Now she had fallen in love with him – a white man – exactly what her mother warned her against. What would keep Jim from leaving her and Patusan one day? The world "out there" had always been one vast Unknown to her, and then Jim came to her from that vast Unknown, as did Marlow now. Marlow sensed that she felt that he could – and would – "with a word whisk Jim away – out of her arms." He was overwhelmed by her breathless urgency to keep Jim.

Marlow was touched by Jewel's innocence and her youth, as well as by her "wild flower" beauty and by her tremulous fears. To her, Marlow clearly stood for the frightening void of the Unknown. If he had not come for Jim, Jewel asked, why had he come? Marlow tried to explain that he had come because of friendship and because of business. But the girl was firmly convinced that he had come for Jim. Marlow said that she must trust Jim: he would never leave her. Marlow also told her that she was the only one in Patusan who doubted Jim's word.

Jewel said that Jim swore never to leave her, but she could not believe him. His promise was not enough. And yet she feared for his life if he stayed. She had even begged him to go. But after Jim killed a man and sent three others back to Sherif Ali, he and Jewel fell in love "under the shadow of a life's disaster." Jewel said that she feared dying like her mother – that is, dying of sorrow because of a man. And even if Jim did swear never to leave her, what made his vow any more honorable than any other white man's vow? Was Jim, she asked Marlow, any different from other men? Marlow answered Jewel. He said that yes, Jim was different. Was Jim, Jewel asked, more brave? More true?

Marlow tried to discover what Jim had told the girl about his past, but he could not. Seemingly, Jim had told her only that once, long ago, he was "afraid." Jewel beseeched Marlow to tell her what it was that Jim was afraid of. How could she battle this ghost in Jim's past? Jim had told her that "the world out there" did not want him; was it true, she asked. Marlow answered that yes, it was true.

Jewel continued to ask questions about Jim until Marlow exasperatedly shouted that Jim was "not good enough" for the world. Jewel was stunned. Those were the same words that Jim had uttered when he had told her why he had to stay on at Patusan. "You lie!" she cried out to Marlow.

Hearing footsteps, Marlow slipped away.

Commentary

These chapters are essentially devoted to the love that developed between Jim and Jewel, and the difficulties that Jewel encountered when she tried to believe Jim and trust him – in spite of the fact that everyone else in the village trusted him completely.

In Chapter 31, we go back in narrative time to a point before Jim blew up Sherif Ali's fortress; we return to a night when four of Sherif Ali's men attempted to kill Jim. It was the first night that Jim discovered that the girl, Jewel, had constantly kept a vigil over him while he was sleeping, thus indicating to him her deep concern for him.

At first, when Jewel came to him, Jim thought that she was in trouble; then he was annoyed when she told him that his life was in danger. He had heard this fear expressed so many times from so many people that the threat had become boring.

This time, however, Jewel was correct, and we see Jim confronting the charging killer and capturing the three men in hiding. The entire purpose of this scene is to illustrate both to the reader and to Jewel the nature of Jim's courage.

Here, in the face of almost certain death, Jim did not "jump." He held his ground until the last possible moment, and then he fired at the charging killer. By standing his ground, Jim displayed considerable courage; in one sense, he has begun to redeem himself from his jump from the *Patna*. Furthermore, Jim grew in stature in Jewel's eyes.

In Chapter 32, Jim expressed some of the paradoxes of his love for Jewel. First of all, he couldn't leave her because he had become convinced that his very existence was essential for her own continued existence. He was obligated to her. He was, however, troubled that he could never be completely honest with her, partly because she would never believe him if he were to tell her the true reason for his being in Patusan.

That is, Jewel has seen Lord Jim perform outstanding acts of bravery, courage, and defiance; thus, she would never believe him if he were to tell her the true state of affairs. But the colossal irony is that if Jim were to tell Jewel or anyone else about his past, they not only wouldn't care, but they would agree that Jim had done the right thing in saving his own life. This view is what will make it so impossible for Jewel and Tamb' Itam to accept Jim's decision, at the end of the novel, not to "run for his life."

Chapters 32 and 33 present a fuller view of Jewel. When she is alone with Marlow, she questions him about Jim because she can't understand Jim. We see her as an acute, sharp, intelligent woman, but one who is still naive and innocent. She also has deep fears of Marlow's "hold" over Jim, and as Marlow says: "I belonged to the Unknown that might claim Jim for its own at any moment." Jewel greatly fears this great Unknown. Jewel knows that other white men have come, and they have always left after awhile: "They always leave us." Sometimes she thinks that Jim "in his sleep when he cannot see me [will] then arise and go" because even though "other men had sworn the same," yet they *all* have left. The irony of these fears is that, in the ultimate analysis, Jewel is right. In deciding not to flee (not to make a run for his life later on) and in his decision to face death rather than live with her, Jim will be "deserting" Jewel.

CHAPTERS 34 & 35

Summary

The footsteps which Marlow heard that night were Jim's, but Marlow was unable to talk any further with Jewel that night – or with Jim. He left, and as he walked away in the cool darkness of the night, he was awed anew at Jim's plans for a coffee plantation on Patusan, along with all of Jim's other plans and his seemingly inexhaustible energy; Marlow could not understand Jim's optimistic enthusiasm for "ever so many experiments."

Marlow confesses that he stood alone that night long enough to succumb to "a sentimental mood." He felt strange and melancholy, remote and lost. Here he was in Patusan, in this forgotten, obscure corner of the world, where he was privy to terrible secrets, and where a man's destiny was being decided and where a woman's love was breaking her heart.

Marlow knew that the essence of that moment and the emotions of that moment would be lost tomorrow, and even if that moment were remembered, it would never again seem as real as it did at that moment; it would always seem as if it were an illusion. And yet it is that moment which Marlow has tried to recount for his listeners.

Marlow's moment of insight into Jim's destiny was shattered by Cornelius, who bolted out of the undergrowth, "vermin-like" and running toward Marlow, whining and cringing, trying to confide in him. Usually, Marlow says, he was so repulsed by the creature that a quick glance at him had always caused him to slink away. But that night, "I let him capture me without even a show of resistance." Marlow says that he felt "doomed to be the recipient of [Cornelius'] confidences."

Cornelius came immediately to the point. He wanted Marlow to talk to Jim and ask him for "some money in exchange for the girl." He had raised her, and she had been someone else's child. Now he was an old man, and he felt that a "suitable present" (money) should be given to him when Jim decided to "go home."

Marlow insisted that Jim was not preparing to leave; in fact, he said "the time will never come." Jim would never go home, Marlow emphasized. Cornelius nearly went into convulsions when he heard this statement. He cried out that he would be "trampled" by Jim until the day he died. He leaned his head against the fence and began uttering threats and blasphemies in Portuguese, mingled with groans and cries of sickness. It was, says Marlow, "an inexpressibly grotesque and vile performance," and so he departed.

Next morning, as Marlow was leaving, he watched the houses of Patusan disappearing behind him. The trees and the river and the people all disappeared, but their clear-cut, indelible, unchanging, unfaded images were stamped upon Marlow's memory. All of these memories, especially those of the people, are suspended now – flat replicas filed away forever, unchanging. All unchanging, that is, except Marlow's memory of Jim. Marlow can't be certain of his final image of Jim. "No magician's wand can immobilize him under my eyes," he says, because "he is one of us."

Jim accompanied Marlow on the first stage of his journey back to "the real world," and after they landed on a bit of white beach, Jim noticed a fisherman signaling to him and he knew what must be done. Tomorrow, he told Marlow, he would meet with Rajah Allang and discuss the fisherman's problems concerning some turtle eggs, no doubt weighing the fisherman's claim against those of Rajah Allang's men. As Jim said, "the old rip [Allang] can't get it into his head that . . ." and Marlow finished Jim's sentence: ". . . that you [Jim] have changed all that."

The two men shook hands then, and Marlow told Jim that he would be returning to England in a year or so, and Jim asked Marlow to "Tell them . . . ," and then he stopped. "Tell them . . . nothing," he said finally.

Marlow clamored on board his schooner. The sun had set, and the western horizon was a blaze of gold and crimson. He saw two half-naked fishermen talking to their "white lord." As Marlow sailed away, the white figure of Jim, pasted against the stillness of the sea, became only a tiny white speck. And, suddenly, Marlow says, "I lost him. . . ."

Commentary

These two chapters end Marlow's direct association with Lord Jim. The rest of Jim's story will be given to us by reports, documents, and letters concerning Jim, along with Jewel's and Tamb' Itam's reports of Jim.

We hear again that Jewel refuses to believe that Jim is not "good enough" for the outside world, and Marlow's attempts to convince her of Jim's loyalty by his explanations "only succeeded in adding to her anguish the hint of some mysterious collusion, of an inexplicable and incomprehensible conspiracy to keep her forever in the dark."

Marlow was ready to leave because he was now convinced that his earlier views of Jim were the correct ones—that is, Jim had indeed proved to all concerned that "he was one of us," and now Marlow saw that all of his efforts on Jim's behalf and all of his trust in Jim's essential goodness had been fully justified; thus, Marlow was now content to leave Jim to his own destiny, knowing full well that they would never meet again—that is, that he (Marlow) would never return to Patusan and that Jim would never leave Patusan.

These chapters also present more of Cornelius, a villainous man whom Marlow completely misreads. Marlow considers Cornelius to be such a repulsive, spiteful, cringing, insidious insect that he, Cornelius, is not really dangerous. Marlow, in essence, dismisses this obnoxious creature as being "too insignificant to be dangerous." In terms of Cornelius' treachery with "Gentleman Brown" later, we realize that Marlow is *wrong* in his interpretation of Cornelius' "insignificance."

CHAPTERS 36 & 37

Summary

Marlow ends his story. The men drift off the verandah quietly, without queries or comments about Marlow's incomplete story of a white man who chose to go into a dark, savage jungle in order to regain his self-worth.

The question, however, remains: what was the ultimate fate of someone who was "one of them," and yet who was someone who chose to achieve greatness in an alien world, and yet in a world of his own making, a world in which he had accepted enormous responsibility for peace, and for life and death. Only one man of those on the verandah is ever to hear the last of the story.

More than two years later, this man received a thick packet, addressed in Marlow's handwriting. It arrived in the midst of a driving rainstorm on a winter's evening. Inside the packet were four separate enclosures: (1) several pages of close handwriting, pinned together; (2) a loose sheet of paper with a few words in handwriting that the man was not familiar with; (3) a letter from Marlow; and (4) another letter, yellow and frayed.

The man turned first to Marlow's letter. Marlow tells the man who is reading the letter that he (the letter reader) was always reluctant to admit that Jim had indeed "mastered his fate." Moreover, Marlow says, you prophesied that one day Jim would feel disgust with the honor which he had acquired in his "new world." According to Marlow, this man (who now reads Marlow's letter) said long ago that Jim had, in effect, sold his soul for a clean, pure slate that was granted to him by some "brutes"—meaning the brown, and yellow, and black Malay natives.

Marlow writes that Jim himself said two years ago that he had no message for "home"; however, it is clear that Jim *did* make an attempt to send a "message." It is Jim's writing, Marlow says, on the gray sheet of "foolscap" paper.

Marlow says that one of the first things that Jim did after he, Marlow, left Patusan was to carry out a plan of defense for "his people." He had a deep ditch dug and surrounded it with a strong, spiked fence, with Doramin's cannons positioned at its four corners. This fortress was a place of safety, a place where "every faithful partisan could rally in case of some sudden danger." Jim called this structure "The Fort, Patusan." Those words are on the sheet of foolscap, along with fragments of two messages that Jim had attempted to write: "An awful thing has happened" and "I must now at once . . ." And then there is a blotch, as if Jim's pen sputtered.

In the packet, there is also a letter to Jim from his father, the parson, who writes about what each member of the family is doing. It is a comfortable letter, the father talking easily about faith and virtue and cautioning his son "not to give way to temptation." At the moment of "giving way," his father says, one succumbs to "total depravity and everlasting ruin." He admonishes Jim never "to do anything which you believe to be wrong." The letter arrived just before Jim sailed aboard the *Patna*.

The last document is another letter from Marlow; it is the story of Jim's last days, pieced together from fragments which Marlow learned. It reveals what happened to Jim after Marlow left him on the beach. There is pain in Marlow's words as he writes about Jim's fate. He says that he can scarcely believe that he will never again hear Jim's voice, never see "his smooth tan-and-pink face . . . the youthful eyes darkened by excitement to a profound, unfathomable blue."

The key figure in Jim's tragic end was named Brown, "Gentleman Brown," as he called himself, even though he had a fierce reputation as an immoral and dangerous buccaneer. Marlow listened to Brown's story as Brown lay dying of asthma in a shack in Bangkok. Jim, Brown said, was nothing more than a "hollow sham," adding that Jim didn't have "enough devil in him" to fight like a man. Brown bragged about having made an end of Lord Jim. Later that night, Brown died.

Marlow says that he learned even more about Jim when he returned some eight months earlier to see his old friend Stein. At Stein's, he saw a Malay native, one from Patusan. It was Jim's "morose shadow of darkness," his bodyguard, Tamb' Itam. Startled at seeing Marlow, Tamb' Itam hung his head, and then he blurted out, "He would not fight. He would not fight."

Marlow found Stein studying his butterfly collection, and Stein asked Marlow to come and talk to Jewel. In particular, he asked Marlow to ask her to forgive Jim.

Jewel was sitting in Stein's big reception room, dressed in white. The crystals of Stein's chandelier above her twinkled like icicles. Marlow sensed Jewel's remote, icy despair. Seemingly, she was "frozen" with unforgiving anger toward Jim. Despite Jim's promises, he *did* leave her. He could have fought for his life; he could have fled. But he did neither. He chose, deliberately, to die. Thus, according to Jewel's logic, Jim *chose* to leave her. "He was like the others. . . . He was false," she says.

At this point, Marlow's letter ends, and the story continues on the sheets of paper that Marlow included, piecing together informa-

tion which he gathered from Brown, from Jewel, and from Tamb'
Itam.

Commentary

This chapter presents a type of transition from the earlier narration by Marlow to a type of narration presented through documents
and letters, "pieced together by" Marlow and sent to one of the men
on the verandah who listened to Marlow's story. The time of the
receipt of the packet is some two years after the events of the last
chapter.

Conrad's use of these narrative devices and the introduction of
an anonymous recipient of this material is perhaps the most awkward
and unaesthetic aspect of the novel. This method of bringing the novel
to a climax is, for the modern reader, terribly distracting and unjusti-
fied as a narrative technique, and the introduction of the anonymous
recipient of the letter is totally unwarranted—we simply don't care
about this person. The whole chapter is out of place.

In Chapter 37, as is typical of this novel, Conrad jumps forward
in his narration, and we hear about the death of Jim before we hear
about the events surrounding Jim's death. We are also introduced to
Gentleman Brown, the instrument of Jim's death.

In Gentleman Brown, we meet the epitome of Jim's nemesis—a
person who reeks of pure evil. At this point, we are not prepared for
someone who thoroughly and irrationally hates Jim for no other reason
than the fact that Jim is a good and honorable man. Had Jim screamed
at Brown, "Hands off my plunder," Brown would have respected him
as another pirate or as another mercenary, but Brown has never before
encountered so perfect and so honorable a gentleman. Thus, Brown
can only respond to Jim with disgust. On his deathbed, Brown is
ultimately pleased that he "paid out the fellow" and that finally he
did "make an end of him after all."

Conrad gives us this information before we see the encounter between Jim and Brown in order to let us know that Jim should have
handled Brown in an entirely different manner. In other words, the
reader thoroughly dislikes Brown after this introduction to him, and
he wishes futilely that Jim would have followed the advice of his
associates who wanted him to destroy Brown.

This chapter also confirms Jewel's earlier fear that Jim eventually
would, like all the other white men, finally leave Patusan. But note

that before meeting Jewel at Stein's house, Marlow meets Tamb' Itam, who cries out to Marlow that Jim "would not fight. He would not fight."

To the incredibly loyal native, Jim's refusal to fight was totally incomprehensible and therefore unforgivable. The same is also true for Jewel: upon seeing Marlow, she immediately cries out that "He has left me . . . you always leave us – for your own ends." She also feels that "It would have been easy to die with him." Jim's death confirms her earlier statements and fears. She could have accepted anything that Jim might have decided to do – *if* his decision had been made with *survival* being uppermost in his mind. Jewel wanted Jim to save his own life, to fight for survival. She could have forgiven Jim anything – except one unalterable fact: Jim deliberately *chose* death over a life with her. Because of this decision, she can never forgive him. The shock and horror of Jim's choice of death and honor over life and love is unfathomable to Jewel. Not surprisingly, it has changed her nature. Jewel has changed from "passion into stone." She has been betrayed by Jim, and she will never understand or ever recover from his betrayal of her.

CHAPTERS 38 & 39

Summary

Marlow's first sentence focuses on "the man called Brown." Brown was the terror of the Polynesian islands; he was a well-known, much-feared, immoral pirate who operated off the Australian coast. He did some gun-running, and he robbed and killed and even maimed people for little or no reason. It was also reported that he once kidnapped the young wife of a missionary. He was infamous for his arrogance and for his uncontrollable temper, and he was particularly contemptuous of men who were weak, "quiet and unoffending."

At the height of Jim's fame as the beloved Lord Jim of Patusan, Brown had a run of bad luck. Finally, he was captured by a Spanish patrol. They intended to imprison him, but when they docked at a small Spanish settlement, Brown and his men stole a schooner and headed through the Straits of Macassar. They planned to take the ship to Madagascar, but first, they had to cross the Indian Ocean and, in order to do that, they needed both food and water. Thus, they anchored off the mouth of the river leading to Patusan, hoping to find provisions there.

Brown and fourteen of his crew headed upriver. When they reached Patusan, they were fired upon, but they were able to secure themselves on a knoll about nine hundred yards from Rajah Allang's stockade. They were far from safe, however. As they looked down into the town, they could see the village swarming with "thousands of angry men." Brown was in utter disbelief at the size of the place.

Jim was away when Brown's party was fired upon. He had been away in the interior for over a week, and Dain Waris was in charge. Dain Waris wanted to kill Brown and his men immediately, but the Bugis were not convinced that it was necessary to massacre the white men. It was a decision that Lord Jim would have to make. They trusted only Lord Jim's judgment. Besides, Dain Waris might be killed. In contrast, Jim was the physical incarnation of Truth; he was invincible. Thus, he had to decide what must be done. And so, in Jim's absence, the villagers crowded into his stockade, much like uncertain children waiting for a parent to return home.

Like Dain Waris, Jewel tried to convince the villagers to destroy Brown's band of pirates, but they would not listen to her. Jewel even had the key to the hut in which five hundred kegs of explosive powder were stored, but no one was willing to initiate such violence. Old Doramin, of course, could have decided the fate of Brown and his men, but he too hesitated; he feared for his son's safety. Nonetheless, he finally ordered that some powder, bullets, and percussion caps be distributed under Jewel's supervision.

Almost immediately, wild and exaggerated rumors began spreading that a large, armed vessel might be moving upriver to aid Brown, so Doramin sent Dain Waris downriver in order to cut off Brown's retreat and to prevent another ship from assisting Brown.

A native called Kassim, a representative of Rajah Allang, arranged for the slimy Cornelius to make contact with Brown's party. Kassim secretly wanted to take over Patusan, and he knew that he could count on Cornelius to help him by telling Brown about the "unusual," white, Lord Jim who "ruled" Patusan. Jim was a man whom Kassim could not understand; he could not figure out how to take the country from him. Jim was not like the other white men he knew. But Brown was another matter. Brown had a criminal nature, and Kassim could manipulate that kind of man—providing Brown was sufficiently tempted to try and take Patusan by force.

Cornelius, of course, hated Jim, and so he tried to make the possibility of conquest seem as easy as possible. Jim, he told Brown, would be a pushover. Jim was an idealist with no real bravery. The natives had been "captured" by the man's charisma, not by his physical courage. Once Jim was dead, Cornelius vowed, the country would belong to Brown.

Commentary

Chapters 38 and 39 present more of Gentleman Brown's background, further showing his corruptness, his evil nature, and his amorality. Brown kills for the sake of killing: he is "a blind accomplice to the Dark Powers." What makes Brown so dangerous is the fact that he "was tired of his life and not afraid of death." In fact, Brown would rather be killed than face the possibility of imprisonment. This lack of a fear of death is what makes Brown such a danger to everyone.

It is ironic that Lord Jim is trusted so thoroughly by the people of Patusan that they will not do anything on their own concerning the fate of Gentleman Brown. Even though Dain Waris and Jewel both want the evil man to be killed, the other natives want to wait until Jim's return. Thus, by the very trust that the natives have for Jim, they place Jim in a position of having to make a decision about Brown's life, a decision which will ultimately bring about the deaths of many people, including Dain Waris and Jim himself.

These two chapters also present the other forces aligned against Jim. Kassim is a bitter and evil person who hates without reason, and Cornelius has long despised Jim and has longed for his death because Jim is so perfect and good. Rajah Allang wants Jim dead so that he can return to terrorizing the natives again. Thus, they are all aligned in their treachery against Jim and the forces for good.

CHAPTERS 40 & 41

Summary

Brown pretended to be interested in Kassim's and Cornelius' proposals, but, in actuality, he was waiting for Jim to return. He was intrigued by the idea of a weak man ruling Patusan. He was also more than a little interested in the reality of "a fort," readymade and waiting for him. He felt sure that he and Jim could work out some kind of arrangement, some kind of plan in which they could "work like brothers." Then, at the proper time, Brown would put an end to Jim, and the land would be his "to tear to pieces, squeeze and throw away."

Marlow tells us that Brown had an "undisguised ruthlessness of purpose." For an example of Brown's loathsome nature, note that he ordered one of his men to shoot a Malay native in cold blood. He wanted the man shot for no other reason than wanting to "strike terror . . . terror, terror, I tell you."

That night, Brown's spirits fell; escape seemed impossible. He knew that his men were outnumbered two hundred to one, and they too were growing restless and fearful. One of them asked permission to get some tobacco. Brown told him to go. But just as the man cried out in delight that he had found some tobacco, a shot rang out and the night air was filled, again and again, with the groans of the wounded man. Six hours later, the incoming tide silenced the moans of the wounded man.

That night, in the stillness, a sonorous voice proclaimed that "between the men of the Bugis nation living in Patusan and the white men on the hill . . . there would be no faith, no compassion, no speech, no peace."

At dawn, a cannon barked briefly. Jim was coming back, Cornelius told Brown. Lord Jim was returning; the cannon was a salute to welcome him. Brown was anxious to talk to Jim, and Cornelius assured him that it would be no problem. Jim, he said, was not afraid of anything. He was like a child; he was a fool. Jim would simply tell Brown to leave "his people" alone, and Brown could easily kill Jim. Then Brown could do "anything you like."

Brown spotted Jim almost immediately. Jim was dressed all in white and was surrounded by "a knot of coloured figures." A contempt, a wish to "try for one more chance—for some other grave" pulsed within Brown when he saw Jim. He waved wildly, and the two men began advancing toward one another until they stood facing each other across the creek. Then Brown jumped the creek. With steady eyes, each man tried to understand the other one before either one spoke.

Marlow is sure that Brown detested Jim at that moment. He is certain that Brown inwardly cursed Jim for his youth, his assurance, his clear eyes, and his untroubled bearing. Jim was the antithesis of Brown's sunken, sun-blackened body and soul. Moreover, Jim had a sense of possession, security, and power. He was not hungry, and he was not desperate; his clothing was pressed and his shoes were whitened.

But Brown knew that Jim must have *something* in his past which caused him to come here, and so when he asked Jim why he came to Patusan, he was elated to see Jim tremble slightly. He had tapped Jim's weakness. Thus, he told Jim that they *both* probably had shady pasts, that they *both* were no doubt running away from something, and that they *both* shared a common guilt.

In effect, he slapped Jim in the face with his taunts, challenging Jim to let him go free and starve, or else to shoot him immediately. This moment, Brown recalled to Marlow, was wonderous; Brown had cornered Jim psychologically. The memory of that moment was sufficient to warm Brown's dying moments. He remembered feeling intensely joyous. He had discovered that he could rattle the "twopenny soul" of Jim, that "confounded, immaculate, don't-you-touch-me sort of fellow."

Commentary

Chapter 40 continues to blacken the picture of Brown, showing him as one of the most detestable characters in fiction, possessing absolutely no redeeming traits. He uses everyone in order to achieve his evil purposes merely for the sake of evil. Like Shakespeare's Iago, he seems to dwell upon evil merely for the sake of evil. For example, he is delighted that there is a fort already built so that he will be able to crush the people of Patusan more efficiently.

At the end of Chapter 40, he is told by Cornelius that Jim is like a child—that he has no fear of anything and that it will be very easy to take anything from him.

Not surprisingly, in Chapter 41, Jim goes to see Brown. From the very first meeting, Brown despises Jim because Jim is clearly loved and trusted by the people of Patusan and because Jim's looks and assurance and youth are in total contrast to Brown's blackened body and his dark, evil soul. Furthermore, Jim displays no sense of fear; he seems entirely self-possessed and confident.

However, as the two men talk, Brown, who is evil but no fool, is soon able to worm his way into the inner nature of Jim. Brown reminds Jim that they are *both* here because of some guilty thing that happened to them in the past, and that they *both* must have done things in the past of which they are ashamed. As Brown says, "I am here because I was afraid once in my life." This, of course, is a terrifying parallel to why Jim is here – that is, once in his life, Jim, possibly out of fear, jumped. And ever since, to the public and to himself, Jim has been convinced that he is indelibly branded as a "coward."

Note that Brown uses the same imagery associated with Jim's jump from the *Patna* – "I am sick of my infernal luck. . . . There are men in the same boat – and by God, I am not the sort to jump out of trouble and leave them in a d——d lurch." These words and illusions serve to remind Jim that a man should not be judged by a single act performed under stress and duress. These comments, as we will see, will lead Jim astray in his judgment of Brown's basically evil nature and will render Jim incapable of acting as a free agent. Jim's inability to see through Brown's evil nature and treachery simply because Brown makes such a parallel analogy to their mutual pasts causes Jim to feel a compassion for Brown which will, in turn, bring about the tragic deaths of Dain Waris and others, including Jim himself.

CHAPTERS 42 & 43

Summary

Brown didn't know precisely what he had come upon in the jungle. But he sensed, intuitively, that Jim was a man with a guilty conscience and was, therefore, pitifully vulnerable. Brown, of course, never expected to confront this sort of man. He supposed that he would have to battle Jim physically for control of Patusan. Of course, he did not tell Jim this. He simply fed Jim's weakness by continuing to speak of their "common blood," the bond between both their minds and their hearts. And at last, Lord Jim walked away, promising Brown either "a clear road or a clear fight."

Cornelius was furious. Why didn't Brown kill Jim? Brown answered that he could "do better than that."

Jim returned and tried to convince Doramin and the other Bugis to allow Brown and his men to return downriver. Doramin was against the idea. Jim then suggested that they call Dain Waris back and allow him to massacre Brown and his men; Jim said that he himself could not do so.

Jim then promised to answer with his life if any harm came to any of the Bugis if they agreed to let Brown and his men leave Patusan. Doramin still did not respond, and Jim told him to call in Dain Waris, for "in this business, I shall not lead." He had to live according to his own code.

Tamb' Itam, Jim's bodyguard, was thunderstruck when he learned of Jim's decision. Jim, in turn, elaborated on his decision: he wanted Brown and his men to be allowed to leave, he said, because that was "best in my knowledge," and his knowledge, he said, had "never deceived you [the Bugis]." At last, most of the men said that they would comply, because, above all, they believed and trusted in the wisdom of Tuan Jim.

Jim realized the immensity of his responsibility. He told Jewel that he was "responsible for every life in the land." Accordingly, Jim wanted no misunderstanding to occur, so he spent the night patrolling the streets. Then he put his own men in Rajah Allang's stockade, which commanded the mouth of the creek. There, Jim intended to remain until Brown and his party passed downriver.

Next, he sent Tamb' Itam downstream to warn Dain Waris that Brown and his men would be passing, and they were to be allowed to proceed without incident. Tamb' Itam asked for some sort of token so that Dain Waris would know that it was Jim himself who had issued this unusual order. Jim gave his bodyguard the silver ring that Stein gave to him long ago.

Jim then sent Cornelius to Brown, telling Brown to use the full tide in the morning, but to be very careful not to provoke the armed men who would be alongside the river. Cornelius also added that one of the men would be Dain Waris, who had initially pursued Brown upriver. Cornelius then told Brown that he knew another way out of Patusan. Brown was interested; he agreed to take this new, secret route, especially if it would, as Cornelius promised, route him *behind* Dain Waris. Then, if "something happened," the people would cease to believe blindly in Lord Jim. "Then," says Brown, "where will he [Jim] be?"

Commentary

In Chapter 42, once Brown has discovered Jim's weak spot, he continues to emphasize to Jim that there is a *common bond* between them — that they both share some kind of *common guilt*. As noted above, Brown is similar to Iago — that is, while being the incarnation of pure evil, he is nevertheless very astute in psyching out his opponent. Brown, Conrad tells us, "had a satanic gift of finding out the best and the weakest spot in his victims," and it did not take him long to discover Jim's weak spot. In fact, Conrad virtually uses Jim's earlier words when Brown asks Jim if Jim "didn't understand that when it came to saving one's life in the dark, one didn't care who else went – three, thirty, three hundred people," and upon asking this question to Jim, Brown brags that he was delighted: "I made him wince."

Of course, Brown's question uses virtually the same words that Jim used earlier to Marlow when he was trying to explain the confusion aboard the *Patna* and the fact that any man in an emergency would reach out to save his own life. Thus, we see that Lord Jim's deep compassion, combined with his lingering guilt over the *Patna* affair, causes him to totally misjudge Brown. Jim's guilt is still so great that he eventually yields to Brown's refusal to surrender his arms, thus leaving Brown and his men with sufficient means to accomplish the forthcoming ambush.

Having now been exposed to Brown's total devotion to evil, we are in a position to know that Jim was wrong in his decision to release Brown, and thus we can once again see how Jim's judgment has been affected by his guilt long before we know of the impending catastrophe.

For example, Jim's defense of his decision to free Brown and his men – "they were erring men whom suffering had made blind to right and wrong" – could so easily apply to Jim himself, for Jim also feels that as he himself once needed a chance to redeem himself, so these cutthroats might also need a similar chance for redemption. Therefore, Jim pledges his life if any of the men should come to any harm – a pledge that later Jewel and Tamb' Itam cannot see any reason to honor.

In Chapter 43, Stein, upon hearing of Jim's releasing Brown, once again calls Jim a "romantic! romantic!" and in this instance, Stein means that the true romantic is forever looking for the innate goodness of man. Jim's altruistic belief in man's innate nobility causes him to be blind to Brown's evilness and thus allows Brown to wreak vengeance upon Patusan.

CHAPTERS 44 & 45

Summary

Brown ordered his men to load on board, telling them that he would give them "a chance to get even with [the Bugis] before we're done." He was answered by low growls.

Meanwhile, Tamb' Itam reached Dain Waris' camp and was immediately taken to Dain Waris, who was resting on a raised couch made of bamboo. Tamb' Itam handed him the silver ring from Lord Jim. Brown and the white men, he said, "were to be allowed to pass down the river."

Dain Waris listened attentively, then slipped on Jim's ring and gave orders to prepare breakfast and make ready for the return in the afternoon. Then he lay back down and watched the sun eat up the mist and the fog.

It was then that Brown took his revenge. It was, says Marlow, "an act of cold-blooded ferocity," and it seemed all the worse later. Brown used the memory of it to "console" himself as he lay on his deathbed.

Brown landed his men on the other side of the island opposite Dain Waris' camp, and Cornelius led the way to the Bugis' camp. The Bugis were in plain sight. No one guessed that the white men knew about the narrow channel behind the camp. At the precise moment, Brown yelled out, "Let them have it," and fourteen shots rang out.

For a moment, not a soul moved. Then blind panic drove them wildly to and fro on the shore like a herd of frightened cattle. Three times Brown's men fired into the Bugis' camp. Tamb' Itam dropped immediately and lay as if he were dead. He told Marlow that after the first volley of shots, Dain Waris raised up from his couch and received a bullet in his forehead. In a few minutes, the white men vanished.

A month later, three parched, glassy-eyed, whispering skeletons, one of whom said his name was Brown, were picked up in the Indian Ocean. Brown, of course, lived and was interviewed by Marlow.

Tamb' Itam told Marlow that Brown did not take Cornelius with him. Cornelius was seen running among the Bugis corpses, uttering little confused cries. Tamb' Itam caught him and stabbed him twice. Then Cornelius "screeched like a frightened hen," Tamb' Itam says, and so he shoved his spear through him and "life went out of his eyes." Immediately thereafter, Tamb' Itam left for the fort to report to the Bugis what had happened to Dain Waris and his men.

The town of Patusan had a festive air. The women were crowded together in throngs, waiting for the return of Dain Waris and his men. The city gate was wide open.

Tamb' Itam was panting and trembling when he finally reached the town. He saw Jewel, and he mumbled half-coherently to her what had happened during Brown's ambush. Then he ran to Jim's house. Jim was sleeping, but when he saw the confused state that Tamb' Itam was in, he wanted the truth: was Dain Waris dead?

When he learned the tragic news, he immediately gave orders for Tamb' Itam to assemble boats, but Jim's bodyguard told him that after Dain Waris was killed, it was no longer safe for Jim's "servant to go out amongst the people." Jim understood. His world had fallen in ruins. Everything was lost – particularly the confidence that the Bugis had once placed in Jim. Loneliness closed in on Jim. The people had trusted him with their lives, and he had failed them. There was much weeping among the people, but there was more anger within them.

The sun was sinking above the forest when Dain Waris' body was brought into Doramin's compound. The body was laid under a tree, and all of the women began to wail, mourning in shrill cries and screaming in high, singsong lamentations.

Both Tamb' Itam and Jewel urged Jim either to make a stand or to try to escape, but Jim refused. "I have no life," Jim told Tamb' Itam and Jewel. The girl begged Jim to fight, but Jim could not. "Forgive me," he told Jewel, but she could not. "Never, never!" she screamed after him. Neither she nor Tamb' Itam could understand Jim's code of honor.

Jim went to old Doramin and told him that he had come "in sorrow . . . ready and unarmed." Doramin struggled to his feet, helped up by his attendants, and as he rose, the silver ring that he had taken off Dain Waris' finger slipped off his lap and rolled forward toward Jim's feet. Here was "the talisman that had opened for him the door of fame, love, and success."

Jim looked up and saw that Doramin was aiming a pistol directly at his chest. He looked at the old *nakhoda* with "proud and unflinching" eyes. Doramin fired, and Jim fell forward.

"And that's the end," writes Marlow. Even today, Jim remains a mystery to the girl and to Tamb' Itam. But, to Marlow, Jim is not a total mystery. It is true, Marlow says, that Jim passed away "under a cloud, inscrutable . . . and excessively romantic," for not even in his boyhood days could Jim have dreamed such a romantic destiny for himself – and yet that is exactly what he wanted most in life. But ultimately, Marlow said, Jim was not so different. He was, still, even at the end, "one of us."

Commentary

These last two chapters are filled with more action per se than any of the other chapters. We see the attack, the panic caused among the Bugis, the death of Dain Waris, Tamb' Itam's killing of Cornelius and then his quick flight back to Lord Jim, and after Jim's confrontation with Jewel, concerning whether or not to fight, we see Lord Jim go to meet Doramin with the full knowledge of his impending death.

These final chapters show the penultimate treachery of "Gentleman Brown"—his "act of cold-blooded ferocity." What happened, Marlow says, was a lesson—"a demonstration of some obscure and awful attribute of our nature which, I am afraid, is not so very far under the surface as we like to think." Marlow seems to be implying that just as all men are capable of "jumping" (as Lord Jim did aboard the *Patna*), likewise, all men are also capable of some sort of treachery, as performed by Brown. Certainly, Brown himself implied the same theory to Lord Jim, an idea so unnerving that it caused Jim to fail to see Brown's treachery clearly. However, Brown exceeds all decency when he gloats on his deathbed about the havoc that he wreaked upon Lord Jim. In his last moments on earth, Brown rejoiced that Lord Jim was ultimately killed.

When Lord Jim climbs up to Doramin's village to face certain death, he climbs back all of the way that he had "jumped" when he deserted the *Patna*. Jim has conquered fear and shame. He has discovered the chance he waited for, the opportunity to restore to himself his own vision of himself.

Jewel can never understand Jim's decision not to fight and as we have seen earlier at Stein's, she will never forgive Jim because she fully believes that he, like all white men, has deliberately deserted her. Her last words to him as he walks toward Doramin are: "You are false!" She screams these words to Jim, who asks her forgiveness. "Never! Never!" she calls back. Unfortunately, Jewel will never understand Lord Jim's moral position. He had no choice. Morally, Jim *had* to prove his worth to *himself*; fighting had nothing to do with the honor which he had to try and find within himself.

Jim promised safety for his people if they would let Brown go, and he offered his life as proof that they could trust Brown. Now Dain Waris and many others are dead. Jim had to offer his own life in payment. He was a Lord to his people, and he had to give his life when it was necessary. This time, Jim did not flee, and he did not jump.

He had conquered fear and shame, and he met death as a hero would. He made a bargain with the human community, a community he once deserted, and he paid for its trust with his life. At last, Jim became the master of his own destiny.

QUESTIONS AND IDEAS FOR REVIEW

1. What is Marlow's narrative purpose in the novel?

2. What dramatic effect is gained by having an unidentified narrator tell Jim's story until he jumps from the *Patna*?

3. What is the moral wrong that Jim believes he has committed?

4. Define the word "dilemma"; what is Jim's dilemma?

5. Discuss Marlow as a father-figure to Jim.

6. What is Jim's final, redeeming act of courage? Define the word "courage" in relation to your answer.

7. Does Jim find "redemption" in Patusan? Define the word "redemption" in relation to your answer.

8. Discuss the terms guilt, responsibility, duty, courage, cowardice, and honor in terms of Jim's life.

9. Discuss the symbolism and/or irony in Jim's wearing white clothing.

10. Can any of Jim's reactions be explained in terms of the details of his childhood from the clues that are revealed to us?

11. Which is more important to Jim—justifying himself to the world? Or justifying his actions to himself?

12. What does Stein mean when he calls Jim a "romantic"?

13. If Jim is "one of us," is Marlow a romantic?

14. In terms of Stein's symbolism, is Jim a butterfly or a beetle?

15. What role does Jewel play in Jim's life?

16. Describe Jim's relationship with Tamb' Itam.

17. What causes Jim to trust Brown?

18. Discuss the symbolism of the silver ring.

19. Trace Conrad's use of light and darkness throughout the novel.

20. Why did Jim choose to try and find forgiveness in a dark, wild, isolated pocket of mankind?

21. Outline your ideas for a short essay on the "jump motif" in this novel.

SELECTED BIBLIOGRAPHY

ALLEN, JERRY. *The Thunder and the Sunshine: A Biography of Joseph Conrad.* New York: Putnam, 1958.

BAINES, JOCELYN. *Joseph Conrad: A Critical Biography.* New York: McGraw-Hill, 1960.

BOYLE, TED E. *Symbol and Meaning in the Fiction of Joseph Conrad.* The Hague: Martinus Nijhoff, 1964.

CARROLL, WESLEY. "The Novelist as Artist." *Modern Fiction Studies,* I (February 1955), 2-8.

FRASER, G. S. "*Lord Jim:* The Romance of Irony." *Critical Quarterly,* VIII (Autumn 1966), 231-41.

GOSE, ELLIOTT B., JR. "Pure Exercise of Imagination: Archetypal Symbolism in *Lord Jim.*" *PMLA,* LXXIX (March 1964), 137-47.

KRAMER, DALE. "Marlow, Myth, and Structure in *Lord Jim.*" *Criticism,* VIII (Summer 1966), 263–79.

KRIEGER, MURRAY. "Joseph Conrad: Action, Inaction, and Extremity." In his book *The Tragic Vision: Variations on a Theme in Literary Interpretation.* New York: Holt, Rinehart and Winston, 1960.

McCANN, CHARLES J. "Lord Jim vs. the Darkness: The Saving Power of Human Involvement." *College English,* XXVII (December 1965), 240–43.

MOSELEY, EDWIN M. "Christ as Tragic Hero: Conrad's Lord Jim." In his *Pseudonyms of Christ in the Modern Novel: Motifs and Methods.* University of Pittsburgh Press, 1963.

MUDRICK, MARVIN, ed. *Conrad: A Collection of Critical Essays.* Englewood Cliffs, New Jersey: Prentice-Hall, 1966.

SCHNEIDER, DANIEL J. "Symbolism in *Lord Jim:* The Total Pattern." *Modern Fiction Studies,* XII (Winter 1966–67), 429–40.

TANNER, TONY. "Butterflies and Beetles: Conrad's Two Truths." *Chicago Review,* XVI (Winter–Spring 1963), 120–40.

TINDALL, WILLIAM YORK. "Apology for Marlow." In Robert C. Rathburn and Martin Stenmann, Jr., eds., *From Jane Austen to Joseph Conrad: Essays Collected in Memory of James T. Hillhouse.* Minneapolis: University of Minnesota Press, 1958, 274–85.

WILEY, PAUL L. *Conrad's Measure of Man.* Madison: University of Wisconsin Press, 1954.

WRIGHT, WALTER F. *Romance and Tragedy in Joseph Conrad.* Lincoln: University of Nebraska Press, 1949.